Discover Your Giftedness

Discover Your Giftedness

Mels Carbonell, Ph.D.

Uniquely You Resources
PO Box 490
Blue Ridge, GA 30513
Phone: (706) 492-5490
E-mail: drmels@myuy.com
Web site: www.myuy.com

Discover Your Giftedness

Dedicated to my wonderful wife,
Phyllis A. Carbonell,
whose encouragement and help in the
ministry has made this book possible.

Scripture references are from the New King James
Version and the original King James Version. Some of the
references have been paraphrased.

Dust Cover design by Herb Paynter

ISBN 1-888846-00-3

First Edition

Contents

What is Uniquely You?

Uniquely You is a Christ-centered, Bible-based ministry dedicated to empowering and equipping Christians through discovering their giftedness. Uniquely You specializes in the Science of Human Behavior from a biblical perspective.

Results-oriented training and proven resources are now available to help churches improve their effectiveness. Seminar formats and schedules are individually designed to fit each church's needs.

The most popular seminars are:
- *Discover Your Giftedness (DYG) Seminar*
  (church wide training usually conducted on Sunday afternoon or Saturday all or half day)
- *NEW Something More Seminar*
  (for church members and staffs to grow beyond giftedness to godliness)
- *NEW Discover Your Giftedness Seminar for Teens*
  (Exciting half or full day of training designed for teens)
- *Basic Certification Training —*
  (for staffs and lay leaders usually conducted week days)
- *NEW Specialist Certification Training*
  (5 NEW Seminars focusing on certifying specialists)
- *Advanced Certification Training*
  (for professional trainers and consultants)

Uniquely You also specializes in training trainers, consultants, and personal coaches to be more effective. We offer several training opportunities; such as — Church Assimilation, Leadership Training, Wellness Dynamics, Human Relations, and Human Behavior Science. Each training is designed to focus on popular personal and corporate development needs. You don't have to be a natural public speaker or presenter. There are opportunities available to fit your personality and training style.

You may want to just learn how to conduct training using Human Behavior Science resources; such as, our Uniquely You and Discover Your Giftedness Profiles. Or you may want to learn how to become one of our presenters and conduct training in churches and/or businesses. We can help you decide how to set up your own ministry/business.

Our Advanced Certification Training format will certify you to become one of our presenters. Or we can show you how to design your own business plan and organization. We can also give you names, addresses, and phone numbers of customers who have ordered our resources as good leads for possibly scheduling seminars in their churches or businesses.

We are especially excited about our new Specialist Training and Consulting. These seminars are usually conducted on a Tuesday during the day as a breakout session. Everyone will have their choice of attending our most popular Church Assimilation Specialist Seminar or another Specialist Training Seminar. These seminars are designed for those who have already attended our Basic Certification Training and want to go to the next level of competency and credentialing.

Everyone who attends the second day of Specialist Training will now receive an additional certificate and special recognition for completing their Specialist Training.

Uniquely You focuses on helping others succeed with their people effectiveness needs. Whether it's conducting training, personal consulting, providing resources, or just improving your own personal development, Uniquely You can help you!

Go on the internet to our Web site at *www.myuy.com* for more information.

Preface

Not only was this book designed to help believers identify and understand their giftedness in Christ, it also was written to teach them how to exercise their giftedness. So much has been written on the subject of gifts, but nothing to my knowledge has ever addressed the combination of spiritual gifts and personality types.

Many people are confused because they only hear about one or the other. As believers, we need to look at both of these motivations and how they affect our behavior.

Spiritual gifts are the supernatural motivations we receive at our new birth in Christ. Our personality types are the natural motivations we receive at conception. Both of these complement one another. However, there are times when these two motivations also can contradict each other.

There are Christians who have conflicting motivations. This may seem odd, but it is simply the unique way that God works in the lives of His children; hence, we are uniquely created! Every child of God is endowed with unique gifts that motivate and influence everything he or she does.

We are God's "jewels"—diamonds in the rough that He is in the process of molding and shaping for His glory. Each chapter in this book also offers a jewel of insight for us so that we can learn to display God's handiwork through our lives.

Exercising our giftedness—spiritually and naturally—helps us fulfill our calling in life. This is because God gave us spiritual gifts in order to glorify Him. We will never be happier than when we identify and use our giftedness for His purposes.

As we grow closer in our relationship to the Lord, we discover that our unique personalities affect our relationships with others. Identifying and learning how to control our personalities can make the difference in the quality of our lives. This is where we learn that human behavior science needs to complement God's truth in the Scriptures. Remember that science and the Bible are both God's revealed truths.

Human behavior science is the formal study of why normal people do what they do. It is the science of human behavior developed from research. It has been categorized so that we can better understand others and ourselves. However, it should never take the place of the Holy Scriptures. Behavioral science provides practical insight into how we can solve our problems with others, but this cannot be done successfully if we choose to leave God out of the equation.

Most of the problems we face involve people, especially those closest to us. Discovering our giftedness, along with understanding biblical conflict resolution, is valuable in helping us to learn how to solve interpersonal problems God's way.

This book runs on two tracks by answering two vital questions: Where do we fit best in the ministry of our church? And how do we avoid and resolve conflicts once we get involved in church? We shouldn't study one without the other. Both are imperatives which help us improve our effectiveness for Christ.

You may want to use this book as a leader's guide to prepare and teach a class or small group. You may also want to simply use this book for your own personal development. Regardless of your interest, you are to be commended for pursuing this study. It could be one of the most enlightening, challenging, and encouraging studies you will ever have.

Welcome To An Exciting Discovery

Everyone is divinely designed! The Bible tells us that we are "fearfully and wonderfully made" (Psalm 139:14). The truth is: we are gifted individuals! God has created each one of us with a natural "bent" of thinking, feeling, and acting that is unique.

Each one of us has a distinctive personality that makes him or her special in the eyes of God. Unfortunately, however, this does not include only good characteristics. The Bible tells us that we have "sinned and fallen short of the glory of God" (Romans 3:23). Therefore, we need a Savior just as we need one another. We also need to learn how to guard our "strengths" and the "uniqueness" that God has given us, especially when we are relating to others.

In writing this book, my sincere desire is that all who read it will not only come to know others better but more importantly will come to know the One who has created us for His glory. So, I must tell you that there is a prerequisite to gaining the full benefit of what I have written in this book: you must first come to a point where you realize your personal need of Jesus Christ as your Savior and Lord. Once you have done this, He will apply the truths of this book to your heart and life. Not only will you begin to enjoy the life that He has given you, but you will discover that you can walk through each day with fresh hope and security because you are not walking alone. You are walking hand-in-hand with Him, and He will show you how you can enjoy life as only He has intended.

If you have never accepted Him as your Savior and you are unsure of your eternal future, you can change all of this right now. Coming to know Jesus Christ is simple. In fact, it is so simple that many people miss it and in doing so miss the greatest opportunity of all. The Bible is clear concerning our "lostness" and need for salvation. The apostle Paul writes, "For the wages of sin is death, but the gift of God is eternal life through Jesus Christ our Lord" (Romans 6:23). If you recognize you need Him, you are ready to receive God's greatest gift—one that is given freely and one that fully displays His unconditional grace and mercy. It is the free gift of eternal life. "For by grace you have been saved through faith, and that not of yourselves; it is the gift of God, not of works, lest anyone should boast. For we are His workmanship, created in Christ Jesus for good works, which God prepared beforehand that we should walk in them" (Ephesians 2:8-10).

Simply put your complete faith in what Christ did at Calvary is what saves you from the wages of your sin—believing that He died on the Cross to pay for all your sins and rose again to prove His unconditional love for you. The gospel of Christ is the "good news" because it sets you free from your lost condition. (1 Corinthians 15:1-4) On the authority of God's Word, you can now know you have eternal life! The apostle John writes, "And this is the testimony: that God has given us eternal life, and this life is in His Son. He who has the Son has life; he who does not have the Son of God does not have life. These things I have written to you who believe in the name of the Son of God, that you may know that you have eternal life, and that you may continue to believe in the name of the Son of God (1 John 5:11-13).

God does not stop with the gift of salvation! He has even more in store for you as you seek to know Him personally and walk through this life with Him each day. Once you trust Christ as your Savior, you are doubly blessed because you also receive spiritual gifts that have the ability to motivate you supernaturally.

Your spiritual gifts are reflected in the way you think, feel, and act with a special enablement and endowment from God. Just as there are different gifts of the Spirit, there are also different people doing different work for the Lord. No Christian has been given all the spiritual gifts of God. One person may have one gift and another person will have a totally different gift. The key to gaining the maximum benefit from your spiritual gift is learning not to want someone else's gift, but instead to be content with the gift that God has given you and to realize that you need others in order to operate fully as a part of the body of Christ.

Every person is important. Each one of us is needed because everybody is somebody in His body! In Ephesians, Paul writes that we are "fitly joined together," with "every joint supplying to the needs of the body" (v. 4:16). For those who already have a personal relationship with God, I pray you will learn more about the filling (controlling) power of the Holy Spirit. The bottom line is God mastering our giftedness, rather than our giftedness controlling us.

My desire in writing this book also is to help you learn more about human behavior science from a biblical perspective. *Human behavior science,* in a nutshell, studies behavior that is observable and predictable.

Having been won to Christ through scientific confirmation of the Bible, I'm not afraid to search for truth outside of the Bible.

Believing all truth is God's truth, I know true science will never contradict His Word. But we must be careful in our search.

Human behavior science is very appealing to humanists. However, humanism, which celebrates the importance of man, is not biblical. God, not man, is most important in life, and in order to live this life the way God intended, we must guard against any so-called science that places man in a position that is not only above God but is at the center of life.

Once you understand the importance of God as the complete focal point of your life, you can grow toward spiritual maturity and biblical personal development. This book will help you and others in that growth process.

It is my prayer that God will richly bless as you discover your giftedness in Christ.

Discovering Your Giftedness Is Biblical

Jewel 2

Every man has his proper gift of God. 1 Corinthians 7:7

Being gifted is nothing new. It is as old as the Holy Scriptures. Identifying and understanding our giftedness is not a modern psychological discovery. It's an ancient truth for modern times!

There's also a misconception that certain gifts are better than others. There are now "gifted programs" in many schools, suggesting that the gifts that some students have are more important than those of their peers.

The truth is that every child is gifted—naturally. And every child of God is also gifted—supernaturally. God gives every person a good gift—his or her personality at conception. Additionally, God gives everyone who trusts Him as Savior the exact gifts he or she needs at new birth.

• God only gives perfect gifts—"Every good gift and every perfect gift is from above" (James 1:17).

• God gives gifts to us so that we might be the "firstfruits of His creation" (James 1:18). In other words, we are obviously special to God because He made our giftedness a priority in creation.

The psalmist reminds us, "It is He who has made us and not we ourselves" (Psalm 100:3). Scripture also reveals and underscores God's truth about our lives: we are "wonderfully made" (Psalm 139:14).

Our giftedness reflects the unique way we think, feel, and act. It's the way God made or "wired" us. We all have God-given personalities that affect our natural motivations. As Christians, we also have spiritual gifts that influence our supernatural motivations. Identifying our giftedness can be exciting and enlightening.

Society and human nature often make people feel as though they are not gifted. Some may doubt the idea that they are special, but this is not true. Actually, everyone is gifted. We may not feel special, but we are—not because of what we do or say but because of who lives in us and who is motivating us through the gifts of His Spirit.

God doesn't make any junk!

Without a doubt, many people suffer from poor self-images. Somewhere along the line, they have believed a lie and thought that they have not been gifted by God to do anything. This thought of not being gifted is difficult for them to accept. Beginning early in life, we are influenced by the idea that some people are special and others aren't. However, regardless of I.Q. or special abilities, every child of God needs to understand that he or she is special.

Our society has been drilled on achieving results, but God looks at the heart. He is not worried about our achieving the highest position in life. Instead, His concern is that we learn how to walk with Him each day in total devotion. Once we learn how to love Him, we will know how to love others and our gifts will come shining through—not so others can praise us but so they also can learn how to praise God.

Identifying our natural motivations and giftedness helps us feel better about ourselves. But this doesn't mean that we are "sufficient unto ourselves" (2 Corinthians 3:5). No matter how gifted we may feel, we still need God. If we forget this, we will head straight into deep trouble. Our giftedness doesn't negate our need for a Savior. It does not remove our guilt and need for God's forgiveness. The Bible is clear concerning our "lost" and empty condition apart from Christ.

The prophet Isaiah tells us "all we like sheep have gone astray" (53:6). Just as sheep need a shepherd, we need help with our lives. We especially need forgiveness, peace, and purpose, which only God can provide. Divine direction only comes when we trust Christ as our Savior and allow Him to be our Shepherd in life.

Once we settle our eternal destiny and relationship with God, then we are able to deal with our difficulties here on earth. We can now control ourselves and improve our relationships with others. Becoming a Christian has so many benefits.

Every believer is blessed with certain spiritual gifts. No one has all the gifts. God gave different gifts to different people so that we would need each other as we live our lives for Him. Romans 12:3 teaches, "Don't think more highly of yourself than you ought." God made each part of the body to function separately, yet dependent upon the rest of the body. He has made us to operate as the body of Christ in the same way. The arm needs the elbow and the foot needs the leg. One cannot function without the other and the same is true of our roles in the body of Christ.

Identifying our spiritual giftedness is key to understanding our function in the church. The Lord desires to bless and benefit us by using our giftedness for His glory, but He wants us to learn how to do this within the context of a body of believers. Therefore, as we learn how to identify and use our spiritual gifts, we will begin to enjoy the life God has given us. We also will enjoy being with others and working alongside one another for God's glory.

In Romans 12:4-8, Paul admonishes members of the early church to be aware of the grace and the spiritual gifts God has given: "For as we have many members in one body, but all the members do not have the same function, so we, being many, are one body in Christ, and individually members of one another. Having then gifts differing according to the grace that is given to us, let us use them: if prophecy, let us prophesy in proportion to our faith; or ministry, let us use it in our ministering; he who teaches, in teaching; he who exhorts, in exhortation; he who gives, with liberality; he who leads, with diligence; he who shows mercy, with cheerfulness."

Scripture confirms that God gave gifts to Christians, and He gave gifted Christians to the church. "And He Himself gave some to be apostles, some prophets, some evangelists, and some pastors and teachers" (Ephesians 4:11).

God gifted all Christians "for the equipping of the saints for the work of ministry, for the edifying of the body of Christ, till we all come to the unity of the faith and of the knowledge of the Son of God, to a perfect man, to the measure of the stature of the fullness of Christ" (Ephesians 4:12-13). Every child of God possesses at least one spiritual gift with which to serve the Lord and His church better.

There are many gifts listed in the Bible. We're going to concentrate on 23 of them. This is not to conclude that the other gifts are not important. The aim of this book is to help you discover your giftedness in a practical and functional way.

Some of the many gifts in Scripture are similar—such as the gifts of helps, hospitality, and serving. They are described in similar terms.

The gift of ruling, administration, and leadership are also similar. They may be described in a similar way, but some lists point out the difference between the gift of administration and ruling and the gift of leadership. We'll take a look at each of these.

One scholar believes there are a hundred different spiritual gifts in the Bible.

Some are unique gifts such as martyrdom. (Revelation 2:13) No one wants to discover he has that gift! Some consider celibacy a gift of the Spirit. (1 Corinthians 7- 8) I'm sure that most of our single adults would not like to identify with that gift.

Once while I was speaking at a single adult conference, a man came to me and said he was upset because he had filled out someone else's spiritual gifts profile and discovered he had the "gift of celibacy." I asked, "What's the problem?" And he said, "I'm married!"

I'm not saying these unusual gifts are not biblical; but for the sake of practicality, I'm going to focus on the gifts most frequently mentioned in the Bible, and most experienced in the Christian community.

The gifts of tongues, miracles, interpretation of tongues, and healing are often controversial. The purpose of our discovery is not to resolve any theological debate that has been continuing for centuries. We simply want to solve the practical and functional problems of the church. We want to focus on these questions: Where do I fit best in the body of Christ? How can I avoid and resolve conflicts once I get involved in a ministry? To help identify our supernatural and natural motivations, we should identify our spiritual gifts and personality profiles.

Assessing your giftedness can be fun and enlightening. Part of the journey toward gaining a firm grasp on our spiritual gifts is also understanding human behavior science from a biblical perspective. One of the goals of this book is to help you understand why you feel or act the way you do in light of your spiritual gift.

While God created us with certain physical characteristics, He also gave us the ability to be emotional as well. Ultimately, our one goal should be to know Christ and become more like Him. Just as Jesus had emotions and behaved a certain way according to the role the Father had given Him, we can learn how to live according to our giftedness.

Understanding "who" we are helps explain "whose" we are!

Some people constantly examine who they are by comparing themselves to others. However, God wants us to learn how to set the focus of our hearts on Him. We should constantly examine ourselves in order to sharpen our focus on His will and way for our lives. Through the study of His Word and prayer, we also can learn why we feel, think, and act the way we do.

Many people want to avoid self-assessment and discovery, but I believe that if we keep our eyes set on Christ and what He has to say about us in His Word, then both of these will lead to obedience and a deeper walk with Him. There is no way to avoid spiritual growth—especially when we are struggling with a certain problem or weakness and we make an effort to seek God's way through the difficulty. He answers prayer and He knows the desires of our hearts.

The path of every search must pass beyond ourselves toward knowing God better. (Philippians 3:10) This study is to simply understand our motivations, while maturing us into effective servants of Christ.

Before we begin, I want to say that I realize that a problem can arise with this type of study, especially if we have never focused on spiritual gifts. Gaining an overview of the different lists of spiritual gifts can help us learn how Bible scholars identify the many different gifts.

Many Christians often ask, "Which spiritual gift list should I use?" I've found that the shorter list in Romans 12 may be easier to teach, but not inclusive. Others think we should focus on more gifts. I like the "Nine Gifts List" from Romans 12 and Ephesians 4.[1]

---

[1] I realize that Saddleback, Willow Creek, and many other churches recognize the "Twenty-three Gifts List." They probably want to be more inclusive and allow for the manifestation gifts in 1 Corinthians 12 in order not to offend charismatic believers. Interestingly, the Alabama District of the Assemblies of God asked me to create a profile using the 23 spiritual gifts combined with the 4 DISC personality types. At the time, I had only published the 7, 9, and 16 combination profiles, but not one based on the 23. I explained to them that the reason I had not published a profile with the 23 gifts was because it is very difficult to deal with the charismatic gifts of tongues, interpretation of tongues, healing, and miracles from a practical perspective.

There are many Christians who don't believe that the charismatic gifts of tongues, interpretation of tongues, healing, and miracles are in operation in this day and age. Many would question where to place someone with these specific gifts in the ministries of the church.

I don't want to deal with the charismatic controversy. Instead, I want to be more practical than theological because every church has its own biblical convictions about spiritual gifts. I want to create simple assessments that would bless any church desiring to have its members involved in its ministries of their churches without getting argumentative. Therefore, I approach the subject of spiritual gifts from the "KISS" perspective—"Keep It Simple, Saints!"

The main purpose of this book is *not* to settle any theological debates, but to help believers get involved in their churches for God's glory and their personal blessing. The following are four of the most popular spiritual gifts lists. We strongly recommend that you go to your minister or church leaders and ask which gifts list they recommend.

Seven Gifts List
(Romans 12:3-8)

This list of spiritual gifts is also known as the *Motivational Gifts*. Bill Gothard popularized this list through his Institute in Basic Life Principles.

> 1. Administration/Ruling
> 2. Encouraging/Exhorting
> 3. Giving
> 4. Mercy
> 5. Prophecy/Proclaiming/Perceiving
> 6. Serving/Ministry
> 7. Teaching

Nine Gifts List
(Romans 12:3-8 and Ephesians 4:11-12)

This list of spiritual gifts is also known as the *Ministry Gifts*. Larry Gilbert and Dr. Elmer Towns popularized this list through their Institute for Church Growth in Lynchburg, Virginia.

This list includes the following gifts:
1. Administration/Ruling
2. Encouraging/Exhorting
3. Evangelism
4. Giving
5. Mercy
6. Pastor/Shepherd
7. Prophecy/Proclaiming/Perceiving
8. Serving/Ministry
9. Teaching

Sixteen Gifts List
(Romans 12:3-8, Ephesians 4:11-12, and
1 Corinthians 12:7-28, 14:1-3)

This list of spiritual gifts is also known as the *Ministry Gifts*. This is the same list popularized by the *Houts Spiritual Gifts Inventory.*

This list includes the following gifts:
1. Administration/Ruling
2. Apostleship/Pioneering
3. Discernment
4. Encouraging/Exhorting
5. Evangelism
6. Faith
7. Giving
8. Hospitality
9. Mercy
10. Knowledge
11. Leadership
12. Pastor/Shepherd
13. Prophecy/Proclaiming/Perceiving
14. Serving/Ministry/Helps
15. Teaching
16. Wisdom

Twenty-three Gifts List
(Romans 12:3-8, Ephesians 4:11-12, and
1 Corinthians 12:7-28, 14:1-3)

This list of spiritual gifts is also known as the *Manifestation Gifts*. This is the same list popularized by Bruce Bugsbee's/Willow Creek's *Networking,* and *Houts/Wagner Modified Spiritual Gifts Profile*.

This list includes the following gifts:
1. Administration/Ruling
2. Apostleship/Pioneering
3. Craftsmanship
4. Creative Communication
5. Discernment
6. Encouraging/Exhorting
7. Evangelism
8. Faith
9. Giving
10. Healing
11. Hospitality
12. Intercession
13. Interpretation
14. Mercy
15. Miracles
16. Knowledge
17. Leadership
18. Pastor/Shepherd
19. Prophecy/Proclaiming/Perceiving
20. Serving/Ministry/Helps
21. Teaching
22. Tongues
23. Wisdom

Review —

Spiritual gifts are supernatural motivations given to every believer. Everyone doesn't receive the same gift or all the gifts. Just as many parts of the human body work together as one, so spiritual gifts are given to the members of the body of Christ to serve as one.

Their purpose is to bring joy and blessings to Christians as they serve the Lord. Once you trust Christ as your Savior, you receive one or more unique ways of thinking, feeling, and acting. Spiritual gifts are divine enablements and endowments that make you a valuable part of the body of Christ.

And He Himself gave some to be apostles, some prophets, some evangelists, and some pastors and teachers, for the equipping of the saints for the work of ministry, for the edifying of the body of Christ, till we all come to the unity of the faith and of the knowledge of the Son of God, to a perfect man, to the measure of the stature of the fullness of Christ. Ephesians 4:11-13

Once you have identified your primary spiritual gifts, you will understand better why you feel, think, and act from a supernatural and godly perspective. You can then enjoy and exercise your giftedness.

Learning without action is wasted knowledge. We need to put feet on our prayers and movement on what we learn. Make a decision today to get involved in the ministry of your church.

If you are already involved, you are a wonderful blessing to your church. God will bless you for it!

Also be sure to ask your minister or church leader which

spiritual gifts list he or she prefers. Don't think you need to understand or accept all the gifts relevant for today or that all the gifts are necessary for your church. Keep this study simple and practical!

You may identify your spiritual gifts profile over the internet any time day or night by going to ***www.myuy.com*** and click on UY Profiler. Or you may order your choice of 4 spiritual gift lists Uniquely You Profile (paper instrument) by phoning (800) 501-0490.

In our next lesson, we're going to look at *Discovering Your Supernatural Motivations* from a practical perspective.

Discovering Your Supernatural Motivations

Jewel

3

Learning why you do what you do because of the influences of your supernatural motivations is vital to serving the Lord. Sometimes your passions, or God's calling and anointing, supersede your gifts.

You may also be serving in a ministry position that doesn't match your giftedness. This may or may not be a problem. It may indicate maturity and a willingness to do whatever God calls you to do, regardless of your giftedness. Or it may explain why you get frustrated in your ministry.

It may be like trying to put a round peg into a square hole. Finding your best "fit" will often result in more meaningful ministry. Fitting your life to your gifts helps you serve the Lord more effectively, and blesses those you serve.

Scripture admonishes us to endeavor "to keep the unity of the Spirit in the bond of peace. There is one body and one Spirit, just as you were called in one hope of your calling; one Lord, one faith, one baptism; one God and Father of all, who is above all, and through all, and in you all. But to each one of us grace was given according to the measure of Christ's gift" (Ephesians 4:3-7).

Sometimes God calls people to do things they are not gifted

to do. He also doesn't always choose the most gifted or talented. The greatest ability He wants is availability. We must always be flexible and respond to the Lord's leading, rather than only responding to our feelings and thoughts. God doesn't always call the "qualified," but He always qualifies the called. "But God has chosen the foolish things of the world to put to shame the wise, and God has chosen the weak things of the world to put to shame the things which are mighty" (1 Corinthians 1:27).

My Personal Story

I'm humbled to share with you that I almost did not graduate from Miami Senior High School because I nearly failed English. I could hardly read and my grammar was terrible. My excuse was that I learned how to speak Spanish before I spoke English. Looking back, it is easy to see that I was going to have problems. On my first grade report card, my teacher noted: "Mels doesn't pay attention in class nor does he follow directions." My last report card of that first year said, "Mels is going to have problems in second grade." And I did, plus I had problems in the third and fourth grades and right on down the line. In fact, sifting through the evidence, it is easy to see that from a human standpoint, I was not much of an academician, but not from God's vantage point. He always sees potential in every life.

So, the point I want to make is that while I'm not much of an English scholar, God has used me in many ways. In fact, here I am writing this book. I now have 26 profiles published, plus 14 large facilitator's manuals. I'm a good example of how God often chooses the "weak" things of the world to do His work. The same is true of your life.

I really want to encourage you, especially if you feel poorly about yourself or think that you are not gifted, to take time to think and pray about God's design for your life. I don't believe I could have ever written any of my resources if God had not gifted me with the gifts of administration/ruling, plus exhortation/encouragement. Also, He created me so that my personality is very determined and decisive. Writing and publishing have been extremely challenging for me, but I honestly believe God has blessed me because of my perseverance. Anyone can do whatever he seriously believes God wants him to do. Is there a challenge that God has given you but you have been hesitant to try? He has gifted you for service, and He will give you the ability you need to complete the task if only you will trust Him.

God gives every believer special gifts to use for His glory. That makes every Christian special in the body of Christ. Every member is a vital part of God's plan. In the church, "everybody is somebody in His Body!" Every member is a "minister" of God.

Discovering your spiritual gifts is important to fulfilling God's plan for your life. Read through the following descriptions to see which gifts may explain your passion or calling.

Spiritual Gifts Descriptions

The following spiritual gifts may or may not fit your theological position. These gifts are not intended to be exclusive or exhaustive. Choose which gifts you believe are in harmony with your understanding of the Scriptures.

As written earlier, I strongly encourage that you also go to your minister or church leaders and ask them which gifts your church recognizes are in operation today. Always remember, spiritual gifts are not intended to divide the body of Christ, but rather unite believers for the "work of the ministry, for the edifying of the body, and unity of the faith" (Ephesians 4:12-13).

Administration/Ruling

The gift of administration/ruling is seen in those who either like to organize or delegate to others. Compelled by a strong sense of duty, they like to find things for people to do. Unlike the gift of ministry, the gift of administration/ruling focuses on team participation. Those with this gift see the big picture and work to keep everyone on track. Not always personally organized, they prefer delegating tasks. They simply like to evaluate what needs to be done, then design systems or give responsibilities to those who can get the job done. They are gifted to help the group forge forward.

> *In a word:* Initiator
> *Overuse:* Expects too much
> *Goal:* Lead by example, not manipulation
> *Scripture:* Romans 12:8; 1 Corinthians 12:28; Acts 6:1-7

Apostleship/Pioneering

Unlike the apostles of old, who actually saw the Lord and spread God's Word from place to place, apostles today have a clear vision to start new ministries where others may not. They make great church planters and strong leaders. Apostles today have a self- or Spirit-appointed calling to reach out where others may never dare. They demonstrate tremendous abilities in influencing others to follow. They also have contagious and industrious enthusiasm to cross cultural, geographical, and economic boundaries for Christ. God today often uses the gifts of apostles/ pioneers as anointed authorities in their region and ministry.

> *In a word:* Pioneer/Visionary
> *Overuse:* Pushes too hard/Too much authority
> *Goal:* Build deeper and stronger
> *Scripture:* Ephesians 4:7, 11; 1 Corinthians 9:1-2;
>   Galatians 2:8-10; 1 Corinthians 12:28-29

Craftsmanship

The gift of craftsmanship is evident in those who are very handy at making things. They have the unusual ability to design and assemble things. They tend to be more task-oriented. They love to create things that are helpful to others and/or appreciated for their quality. Those with the gift of craftsmanship can be tremendous blessings to those who need special help in putting things together or making things from scratch. They can get too involved in the project and often overlook the people around them. They tend to be perfectionists and specialists in whatever craft they take up.

> *In a word:* Handy
> *Overuse:* Too focused on work and not on others
> *Goal:* Create things to bless others, not glorify self
> *Scripture:* Exodus 31:3; 2 Kings 22:5-6

Creative Communication

The gift of creative communication is obvious in those who enjoy performing or directing drama presentations. They love to express themselves and teach lessons through role-playing and skits. They tend to be very creative and able to act out specific feelings to communicate biblical truths. Those with the gift of creative communication must guard against seeking the spotlight. They make great reflections of the Light of the World, which is the Lord Jesus Christ. They also can add a great deal to worship and preaching by creating dramas that illustrate the lessons of the sermons.

In a word: Actor or actress
Overuse: Dramatic expression that leads to self glory
Goal: Teach lessons, rather than focus on talent
Scripture: Psalm 150:3-5; 2 Samuel 6:14-15; Mark 4:2, 33

Discernment

The gift of discernment is evident in those who have unusual abilities to see through a lot of confusion and to pinpoint problems and solutions. They are concerned about right and wrong. They tend to listen well and hear the little and seemingly insignificant things that shed light on a specific need. Those with the gift of discernment are often more serious than others. They distinguish between good and evil, truth and error. They like to ask questions and then give advice. They often relate problems to the violation of biblical principles. They feel strongly about obeying truth and living by the Word of God.

> *In a word:* Listener/Perceiver
> *Overuse:* Too critical or too quick to share
> *Goal:* Get more information before responding
> *Scripture:* 1 Corinthians 12:7, 10b; 2:14

Encouraging/Exhorting

Christians with the gift of encouraging/exhorting find themselves lifting others up. They are compelled to give advice. As counselors, they seem to often have steps of action to share. While prophets declare truth and teachers clarify truth, encouragers like to tell you what to do with truth. They bless others with a strong sense of concern. While they are looking to encourage others, they are sought out as counselors. People find encouragers friendly, understanding, and practical. Encouragers enjoy using their communication skills to share specific insights.

> *In a word:* Encourager
> *Overuse:* Talks too much
> *Goal:* Apply truth, don't create expectations
> *Scripture:* Romans 12:6, 8; Acts 11:23-24;
> Hebrews 10:24-25

Evangelism

Christians with the gift of evangelism feel compelled to win souls. They seem to have the ability to communicate the gospel very effectively. Their concern for witnessing to a lost and dying world is evident. They desire to be involved in ministries to reach people for Christ. The gift of evangelism motivates them to want nearly every message they hear to include the gospel and an invitation to trust Christ. Missions and outreach are important to them. To always be ready to give an answer to every person is his goal. Conversations seem to often turn toward eternal values. The worth of souls and the task of evangelism are most important to the evangelist's motivation.

> *In a word:* Dynamic
> *Overuse:* Zeal without knowledge
> *Goal:* Build disciples, not statistics
> **Scripture:** Ephesians 4:7, 11; Acts 8:26-40; Luke 19:1-10

Faith

The gift of faith is often found in those with the obvious ability to trust God in the most adverse circumstances. Every Christian has a measure of saving faith, but those with the gift of faith have a deeper dependence upon God and His Word. Romans 10:17, "Faith comes by hearing and hearing by the Word of God," is their favorite Bible verse. The gift of faith is seen in those who believe strongly in the presence and power of God. They tend to stretch the faith and commitments of others. They encourage others to act upon their faith and challenge everyone to increase their faith.

> *In a word:* Optimist
> *Overuse:* Overly trusting and often proud of their faith
> *Goal:* Combine faith with works/learn to be patient with
> others
> *Scripture:* 1 Corinthians 12:7, 9; Matthew 8:5-16;
> Hebrews 11:1

Giving

Givers tend to be seriously concerned about financial matters. The gift of giving also involves the "gift of getting." Givers are sensitive to how money is spent and saved. Those with the gift of giving don't always give to the wheel that squeaks the loudest, but to the wheel that truly needs the most grease. Givers have unique financial insights. They serve especially well on boards responsible for maintaining budgets. They tend to be conscientious and conservative. The gift of giving may not always be overtly evident, but a genuine interest in wise stewardship will be clearly seen.

> *In a word:* Steward
> *Overuse:* The power of money
> *Goal:* Sincere stewardship, not financial harassment
> *Scripture:* Romans 12:6, 8b; Acts 4:32-35;
>   2 Corinthians 9:7-8

Healing

The gift of healing is evident in those with the divine power to pray and see people healed. They have unusual faith that God can heal anyone. They prefer worship that emphasizes the healing power of God. Those with the gift of healing are used by God to restore people to wellness. They should focus more on the faith of those needing to be healed, rather than their own faith to heal. They authenticate messages from God's Word through healings. They should remember that God doesn't promise to heal everyone. Developing the faith to carry on is often more important than the healing.

> *In a word:* Restorer
> *Overuse:* Teaching that everyone should be healed
> *Goal:* Focus on God's power and not the gift to heal
> *Scripture:* 1 Corinthians 12:9, 28, 30; Acts 3:1-16;
> Mark 2:1-12

Hospitality

The gift of hospitality is that special interest in opening one's home for food and fellowship, or to just provide a place to stay for someone in need. Those with the gift of hospitality seem to always be ready and willing to invite guests over or offer their homes for a place to meet for any occasion. They love to provide refreshments or prepare meals for individuals or groups. They seldom show irritation over last minute requests to have someone over or to host a group. They tirelessly serve to make people comfortable and encouraged.

> *In a word:* Sociable
> *Overuse:* Take on too much and become worn out
> *Goal:* Provide fellowship without sacrificing family time
> *Scripture:* 1 Peter 4:9-10; Acts 16:13-15; Luke 14:12-14

Intercession

The gift of intercession is found in those with a passion to pray. They feel compelled to intercede on behalf of those in distress. They faithfully petition God on a daily basis for specific needs. They recognize spiritual battles are often won on one's knees. Those with the gift of intercession believe God moves in response to prayer. "Much prayer, much power" is their motto. They should guard against being pushy and feeling superior. They are tremendous blessings to those needing someone to consistently intercede on their behalf. They are the spiritual glue of every church.

In a word: Prayer warrior
Overuse: Neglect other practical needs and responsibilities
Goal: Put "feet on their prayers" and also do what needs to
be done
Scripture: Romans 8:26-27; John 17:9-26;
1 Timothy 2:1-2; Colossians 1:9-12

Interpretation

The gift of interpretation is found in those who can translate what others speak in tongues. They have the unusual ability to glorify God through their miraculous interpretation of what would be otherwise unknown. Those with the gift of interpretation often edify and encourage others through their explanation of what is spoken in other languages. They should guard against adding their thoughts or concerns to what is actually being spoken. They are sometimes very strong with their interpretation, but should always seek to clarify and unify, rather than always prophesy.

> *In a word:* Translator
> *Overuse:* Use translations to push own agenda
> *Goal:* Clarify what is spoken in tongues and build believers
> *Scripture:* 1 Corinthians 12:10, 14:5, 14:26-28

Knowledge

The gift of knowledge is a supernatural revelation of certain facts in the mind of God, which gives instant and specific information that one would have no other way of knowing except from God. This is not an amplification of human knowledge, nor is it a gift of just knowing a lot of things. It is the ability to receive specific truth from the Word of God. Sometimes those with this gift may overwhelm others and bring more attention to their own word of knowledge, rather than the purpose of sharing what God has revealed to them.

> *In a word:* Divine Insights
> *Overuse:* Make others feel inferior or ignorant
> *Goal:* Change lives, rather than impress others
> *Scripture:* 1 Corinthians 12:7-8, 8:1b-2; Mark 2:6-8;
> John 1:45-50

Leadership

The gift of leadership, much like the gift of administration/ruling, is evident in those who demonstrate an unusual ability to influence others. They seem to have an independent determination to challenge and direct others toward a specific goal. They stand out and take stands. Those with the gift of leadership tend to be multitalented, excelling with people and task skills. Often result-oriented and driven, they need to guard their strengths. They also need to be more sensitive and patient with those who do not respond as well or positively as they do. They are great motivators.

In a word: Dreamer
Overuse: Too demanding and impatient
Goal: Lead by example and willingness to be a servant
Scripture: Romans 12:6, 8c; John 13:13-17;
　　　　　　Hebrews 13:17

Miracles

The gift of miracles is obvious in those who do powerful deeds. They have the unusual ability to authenticate through miracles a specific ministry or message of God. God's supernatural intervention through those with this gift will always glorify Him rather than themselves. They express and demonstrate tremendous faith in God's power. They should always explain and teach that God is the source of every good supernatural event. They are only the messengers and means by which God has chosen to act. Miracles are to point people to Christ and not to "miracle workers."

> *In a word:* Powerful
> *Overuse:* Expecting God to always perform miracles
> *Goal:* Trust God, with or without the miracle
> *Scripture:* 1 Corinthians 12:10, 28-29; John 2:1-11;
> Luke 5:1-11

Pastor/Shepherd

The gift of pastor/shepherd is obvious in those who really enjoy leading others in serving the Lord. Unlike the gift of serving/ministry/helps, this gift involves the motivation to lead. Pastor/shepherds are compelled to encourage others to work together for the body's sake. Influencing others to work together is important. Stressing a need for team participation, they emphasize harmony. Untrained laypeople can also have the gift of pastor/shepherd. They see their service as one of maturing others. With a motivation to unite the ministry, they feel strongly about spiritual health.

> *In a word:* Discipler
> *Overuse:* Takes advantage of others' trust
> *Goal:* Strong leadership, not manipulating the flock
> *Scripture:* Ephesians 4:11; 1 Peter 5:2-4

Prophecy/Proclaiming/Perceiving

Prophets today are not exactly like prophets of old. Old Testament prophets spoke the literal Word of God. Today people with the gift of prophecy seem to have the same seriousness and straightforward attitude toward truth. They like to share truth, regardless of what anyone thinks. Prophets today are motivated to confront anyone with what they believe is right. When controlled by the Holy Spirit, the gift of prophecy/perceiving/proclaiming is a powerful tool to reprove, rebuke, and exhort others. Prophets often find themselves pointing the way, declaring a specific truth, or standing up for something significant.

> *In a word:* Bold communicator
> *Overuse:* Fighter
> *Goal:* Declare the truth but don't divide Christians
> *Scripture:* Romans 12:6; Ephesians 4:7, 11;
>   1 Corinthians 14:1, 3; 2 Peter 1:19-21

Serving/Ministry/Helps

When you think of Christians who serve faithfully behind the scenes, you think of those with the gift of serving/ministry/ helps. They are interested in blessing others to serve the Lord. They love to help others. Motivated by a strong sense of need, they feel like "someone has to do it." Caring and concerned for others, they find themselves doing what no one else likes to do. They tend to do whatever is called for. Flexible, they adapt to many challenges. They simply enjoy helping others and meeting needs. Often truly selfless, those with this gift like to be involved.

> *In a word:* Selfless
> *Overuse:* Takes on too much
> *Goal:* Be a servant, not a martyr
> *Scripture:* 1 Corinthians 12:28; Act. 6:1-3; Romans 16:1-2

Showing Mercy

The gift of showing mercy demonstrates genuine sensitivity to suffering. Those with this gift are compelled to help reduce the pain people experience. They are concerned more with the person in difficulty than the reason for the suffering. Focusing on the feelings of those who are hurting emotionally, those with the gift of mercy desire to minister by "being there." When people really need them, they are close by to listen and to offer compassion. Sympathizing and empathizing with those who struggle is their specialty. While others may care more about why, what, when, or how something happened, the person with the gift of showing mercy is interested in "who" needs tender, loving care.

> *In a word:* Caring
> *Overuse:* Too sensitive
> *Goal:* Wise insights, not foolish responses
> *Scripture:* Romans 12:6, 8d; Matthew 5:7

Teaching

Christians with the gift of teaching prefer explaining why things are true. While the prophet declares truth, the teacher explains the reasons why it is true. Interested in research, those with the gift of teaching like to dig into seemingly insignificant details. They enjoy presenting what they discover. Often negligent of the needs of others, they press toward a deeper understanding. They love to study. Searching patiently and persistently, they may miss the obvious. They stretch the limits of learning, setting high standards of education.

In a word: In-depth
Overuse: Digs too deep
Goal: Reveal truth but don't exhaust it.
Scripture: Romans 12:6-7b; Colossians 3:16; James 3:1-2;
2 Timothy 2:2

Tongues

The gift of tongues is found in those with the divine ability to speak other languages. They have the unusual endowment to speak in a language that is not understood by most of those present. They often express themselves spontaneously or in response to what is being preached, sung, or worshiped. They edify God and encourage others through their supernatural message, often with words too deep for the mind to comprehend. Those with the gift of tongues should be careful to not overwhelm others with their gift, but instead speak words "easy to understand," so that the lesson is clear.

> *In a word:* Conduit
> *Overuse:* Disruptive, overbearing, and confusing
> *Goal:* Edify and encourage believers through mostly
> positive messages
> *Scripture:* 1 Corinthians 12:10, 28-30, 13:1, 14:1-33;
> Acts 2:1-11

Wisdom

The gift of wisdom is the unique ability to use knowledge in a practical way. Those with this gift like to combine what they know with a serious reverence of God in order to influence others. They sometimes battle with pride and an attitude of superiority. They need to be consistently humble and exhibit a sense of quietness and slowness before responding. Those with the gift of wisdom are often given some kind of adversity to help them stay in tune with God and His Word. Otherwise, those with this gift will tend to be puffed up. They make great counselors and give tremendous advice. Therefore, they need to stay in constant prayer, asking God for His wisdom.

> *In a word:* Perceptive
> *Overuse*: Speak down to people
> *Goal*: Consistently trust and ask God for wisdom.
> *Scripture*: 1 Corinthians 12:7-8; James 3:13-18

Once you have studied all the spiritual gifts, you can determine which ones fit you best. Don't think that all the gifts are for you. It is very important that you first decide theologically which gifts agree with your interpretation of the Scriptures. Then you should focus on your primary and secondary spiritual gifts.

You may find that after reading through this description that you have more than one spiritual gift. Always keep in mind that the important thing is that you recognize you are a divinely designed and gifted believer in Christ. Your eternal purpose is to glorify the Lord by serving Him through your gifts in His body, and the church you are attending.

Spiritual Gifts Are Given to Bless You!

God gifted you to bring great joy and fulfillment to your life. He also gifted you to benefit your church and ministry. Identifying your spiritual gift/s should help you discover how God wants to use you for His glory. But there is more for you to discover about your giftedness.

You are also gifted with natural motivations—elements of your personality that affect your feelings, thoughts, and actions. Discovering the natural way God made you also helps you understand why you tend to do what you do. That's why in our next lesson we are going to learn about discovering our natural motivations. This is why in our next lesson we are going to look at *Discovering Your Natural Motivations*.

You may identify your spiritual gifts profile over the internet any time day or night by going to ***www.myuy.com*** and click on UY Profiler. Or you may order your choice of 4 spiritual gift lists Uniquely You Profile (paper instrument) by phoning (800) 501-0490.

Discovering Your Natural Motivations

Jewel 4

We receive the skeleton of our personalities from God at conception. He divinely and genetically designed each of us as distinct individuals for a purpose. He also allowed our parents and past experiences (our environment while we were growing up) to divinely engineer us or, better yet, He "designed" us into the persons we are today.

For You formed my inward parts; You covered me in my mother's womb. I will praise You, for I am fearfully and wonderfully made; Marvelous are Your works, And that my soul knows very well. Psalm 139:13-14

The psalmist describes us as being "covered" or knit together in the womb. The word "knit" means we were intricately "embroidered" by God's hand. My mother was a wonderful seamstress. She could do anything with a needle and thread. I still remember that she often embroidered tablecloths and little hankies into beautiful masterpieces.

As a little child I remember how I would look up at the backside of her work and see a bunch of loose strings, which appeared all mixed up without form or fashion. However, when she turned the cloth over and showed me what she was working on, I was always amazed at how gorgeous and intricate the design was. From the back side it was a mess, but from the front side, it was beautiful. The same is true about our lives. When we look at our lives, we may think, "God, I don't know how You can use me. I have made so many mistakes." Remember, He knows the design of your life, and He is not through with you yet!

We may not realize it, but He is fashioning us into masterpieces for His glory. From His viewpoint our lives are beautiful. While we "see through a glass darkly" (1 Corinthians 13:12), God's eyesight is 20/20. He knows the potential our lives contain. When trouble hits or we make horrendous mistakes, all we see is the undersides of our lives. From there, everything looks like a jumbled mess, but God knows what He is doing and He is fashioning us into His wonderful "workmanship" (Ephesians 2:10).

Not only did I learn a lesson about how God sees us as the finished product, but also how my mother influenced me to keep working, even when the strings of life unravel or when our beginnings don't seem very organized.

This is why the environment of our early childhood is extremely important. It influences our personality and the way we view God, others, and ourselves. Nature (God's handiwork) and nurturing (early childhood development) both help to mold and shape us. When we are younger, we don't have the knowledge needed to deal properly with hurts and disappointments as well as achievements and victories. However, we do have a choice in our later development.

When a problem arises, one type of behavior may be perfectly natural, while the other is not. One comes easy; the other does not. Reacting from a human standpoint may seem right, but for the believer the solution comes by being controlled by the Holy Spirit and seeking to do what God wants you to do and not what you naturally want to do. For example, you may be tempted to be angry, but God tells us to bring our troubles and frustrations to Him. Flying off the handle at someone else solves nothing. It can only deepen the problem.

However, we must learn to say, "I don't want to be natural. I want to be supernatural"—to "do all things through Christ Who strengthens me" (Philippians 4:13). This positions us for blessings and service in God's kingdom.

You can say, "I don't want to act like what some people may classify as 'normal,' because when I do, I can be difficult. I want to be 'spiritual.' I don't want to be me. I want to be what God wants me to be!"

Someone has said, "We need to find ourselves." Well, I found myself and I didn't like what I found! Therefore, I realized that I needed to let God conform me into what He wants me to be. The greatest blessing you can receive is the blessing of letting go of your life and letting God take control fully and completely.

I have come to the point where I don't even want to be *real* in the world's way of thinking. Because when I am real or when I'm *the natural me* I may do something without thinking. While the world recklessly wanders in search for the *real person* within, I want a relationship with the One who is conforming me into the image of His dear Son. (Romans 8:29)

Identifying our personalities can help us become more like Christ, but first, we need to understand more about the personalities that our lives contain. While it may seem as though the Bible doesn't specifically address the science of human behavior and personality types, we certainly can learn a lot about it from those who have researched and developed the theories and conclusions over the past 2400 years.

The Four Temperament Model of Human Behavior is attributed to Hippocrates, the father of modern medicine. His scientific research and brilliant observations are widely accepted. Contrary to what critics claim, the Four Temperaments did not hatch from *archaic, pagan Greek philosophy,* but rather from the scientific process that made Hippocrates the respected physician of his day.

DISC Model of Human Behavior Science

William Marston first introduced the DISC Model of Human Behavior in 1928 through his book, *The Emotions of Normal People*. Marston took Hippocrates's Greek titles, which included the choleric, sanguine, phlegmatic, and melancholy personality types, and assigned simple, single D, I, S, and C letters to each. Though there are now many titles to various models, they all have roots from the same basic four temperaments observed 400 years before Christ.

Understanding the four-quadrant model of human behavior can help explain why people do what they do. These insights can make the difference between right and wrong responses, and the best or worst behavior in any situation.

You have a predictable pattern of behavior because you have a specific personality. There are four basic personality types. These types, also known as temperaments, blend together to determine your unique personality.

The closest biblical references or examples of different personality types are only found in Proverbs 30:11-14:

There is a generation that curses its father,
And does not bless its mother. (C-types)

There is a generation that is pure in its own eyes,
Yet is not washed from its filthiness. (S-types)

There is a generation-oh, how lofty are their eyes!
And their eyelids are lifted up. (I-types)

There is a generation whose teeth are like swords,
And whose fangs are like knives,
To devour the poor from off the earth,
And the needy from among men. (D-types).

To help you understand why you often feel, think, and act the way you do, the following preview will summarize the Four Temperament Model of Human Behavior.

"D" BEHAVIOR

Biblical examples: Paul and Sarah
(Active/Task-oriented)
Also known as "Choleric" or "Lion"

Descriptions
Dominant, Direct, Demanding, Decisive

Basic Motivation: Challenge and Control

Desires
• Freedom from control
• Authority
• Varied activities
• Difficult assignments
• Opportunities for advancement
• Choices, rather than ultimatums

Responds Best to Leader Who
• Provides direct answers
• Sticks to task
• Gets to the point
• Provides pressure
• Allows freedom for personal accomplishments

"D" BEHAVIOR

Needs to Learn
- We need people
- Relaxation is not a crime
- Some controls are needed
- Everyone has a boss
- Self-control is most important
- To focus on finishing well is important
- Sensitivity to people's feelings is wise

Biblical Advice
- Be gentle and not bossy—"Wisdom from above is . . . gentle" (James 3:17).
- Control your feelings and actions—"Be angry and sin not" (Ephesians 4:26).
- Focus on one thing at a time—"This one thing I do" (Philippians 3:13).
- Have a servant attitude—"By love, serve one another" (Galatians 5:13).

"I" BEHAVIOR

Biblical examples: Peter and Ruth
(Active/People-oriented)
Also known as "Sanguine" or "Otter"

Descriptions
Inspiring, Influencing, Impressing, Inducing

Basic Motivation: Recognition and Approval

Desires
• Prestige
• Friendly relationships
• Freedom from details
• Opportunities to help others
• Opportunities to motivate others
• Chance to verbalize ideas

Responds Best to Leader Who
• Is fair and also a friend
• Provides social involvement
• Provides recognition of abilities
• Offers rewards for risk-taking.

"I" BEHAVIOR

Needs to Learn
• Time must be managed
• Deadlines are important
• Too much optimism can be dangerous
• Being responsible is more important than being popular
• Listening better will improve one's influence.

Biblical Advice
• Be humble and avoid pride—"Humble yourself in the sight of God" (James 4:10).
• Control your speech—"Be quick to hear, slow to speak" (James 1:19).
• Be more organized—"Do all things decently and in order" (1 Corinthians 14:40).
• Be patient—"The fruit of the Spirit is . . . longsuffering" (Galatians 5:23).

"S" BEHAVIOR

Biblical examples: Moses and Esther
(Passive/People-oriented)
Also known as "Phlegmatic" or "Golden Retriever"

Descriptions: Submissive, Steady, Stable, and
Security-oriented

Basic Motivation: Stability and Support

Desires
• An area of specialization
• Identification with a group
• Established work patterns
• Security of situation
• Consistent familiar environment

Responds Best to Leader Who
• Is relaxed and friendly
• Allows time to adjust to changes
• Allows one to work at own pace
• Gives personal support

"S" BEHAVIOR

Needs to Learn
- Change provides opportunity
- Friendship isn't everything
- Discipline is good
- Boldness and taking risks is sometimes necessary

Biblical Advice
- Be bold and strong—"Only be strong and very courageous" (Joshua 1:6).
- Be confident and fearless—"God has not given you the spirit of fear" (2 Timothy 1:7).
- Be more enthusiastic—"Whatsoever you do, do it heartily, as unto the Lord" (Colossians 3:23).

"C" BEHAVIOR

Biblical Examples: Thomas and Hannah
(Passive/Task-oriented)
Also known as "Melancholy" or "Beaver"

Descriptions: Competent, Compliant, Cautious, and Calculating

Basic Motivation: Quality and Correctness

Desires
• Clearly defined tasks
• Details
• Limited risks
• Assignments that require precision and planning
• Time to think

Responds Best to Leader Who
• Provides reassurance
• Spells out detailed operating procedures
• Provides resources to do task correctly
• Listens to suggestions

"C" BEHAVIOR

Needs to Learn
• Total support is not always possible
• Thorough explanation is not everything
• Deadlines must be met
• More optimism will lead to greater success

Biblical Advice
• Be more positive—"Whatsoever things are lovely, of good report . . . think on these things" (Philippians 4:8).
• Avoid a bitter and critical spirit—"Let all bitterness . . . be put away from you" (Ephesians 4:31).
• Be joyful—"The fruit of the Spirit is . . . joy" (Galatians 5:22).
• Don't worry—"Fret not" (Psalm 37:1).

The graphic on the next page will help you see the Four Temperament Model of Human Behavior as a whole. Study this picture carefully and you can grasp a basic understanding of how each personality tends to respond.

Active/
Task-oriented

"D" — directing, driving,
demanding, dominating,
determined, decisive,
doing

Active/
People-oriented

"I" — inspiring, influencing,
inducing, impressing,
interactive, interested
in people

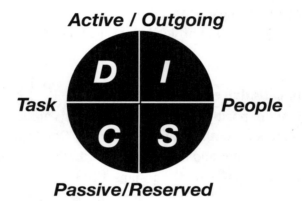

Active / Outgoing

Task   **People**

Passive/Reserved

Passive/
Task-oriented

"C" — cautious, competent,
calculating, compliant,
careful, contemplative

Passive/
People-oriented

"S" — steady, stable, shy,
security-oriented, servant,
submissive, specialist

Get this graphic solidified in your mind and you will be able to recall the DISC Model of Human Behavior much easier.

You may identify your personality profile over the internet any time day or night by going to ***www.myuy.com*** and click on UY Profiler. Or you may order your Uniquely You Profile (paper instrument) by phoning (800) 501-0490.

In our next lesson, we're going to look at *Understanding Your Natural Motivations*.

Understanding Your Natural Motivations

Jewel 5

People are different in many ways, but those differences are most apparent in the things they do—their behaviors. While some remain cool, calm, and collected, others are excitable, enthusiastic, and sometimes explosive. Some are passive and others active. To say one behavioral pattern is good and another bad is wrong thinking. Each one of us responds differently and uniquely to life. However, within the behavioral pattern our responses are often predictable.

Everyone is either active and/or passive!

While the apostle Paul was aggressive, Thomas, one of Christ's disciples, was more passive. Peter liked to be up front, while Andrew, his brother, was behind the scenes.

In John 11:20, Martha is obviously the more active one, while Mary is the one that is much more passive. The Bible does not judge the response of either sister as better or worse. It simply characterizes the two different behaviors.

It is natural for us to gravitate toward roles that fit our personalities. We may find ourselves struggling in roles where our temperaments are tested. Our comfort zones are bordered by the parameters of our personalities. In other words, life is easier when our personalities are not stretched beyond their limits.

My wife and I are good examples of active and passive types. I'm more active and she is more passive. Opposites do attract and they also can "attack," oops, I mean, attract and "attach." We are definitely opposite personalities, but she's the best thing that ever happened to me!

God gave her to me to complete me. Sometimes, I think, "to finish me off!" She has helped to temper and soften my aggressiveness and boldness, while God has used me to improve her assertiveness and to help her not be so shy or quiet.

Do opposites really attract or not?

I noticed a CNN article on the Internet recently stating that human behavior scientists have concluded that opposites do attract. As I read closely, I saw where the scientists had only compared couples with similar values, faiths, and preferences. They wrote nothing about differences in personalities and how opposite personalities tended to attract each other.

Couples with similar values, religions, and preferences DO attract, but they also tend to have opposite personalities according to my research.

The Bible teaches that both active and passive types are appropriate. For example, Mark 16:15 instructs us to "go into all the world and preach the gospel." That is definitely a call for active behavior.

Psalm 46:10 also commands us to "be still and know that I am God." That is obviously a need for passive behavior. Both types of behavior are biblical and both work well when coupled with the appropriate personality type. It is obvious that we need to learn and obey both of these commands.

In fact, God wants us to be both active and passive, but not at the same time. We must be optimistic about His promises and pessimistic about the world's ways—positive about good and negative about evil. The church is full of all types of people. There are active and passive, optimistic and pessimistic, and positive and negative types.

Everyone is also task and/or people-oriented!

There is also diversity between task- and people-oriented behavior. To illustrate this, let's say a "task" type person and a "people" person are both working in a garden. Someone walks up and says, "Hi, how are you—what's happening?" How will the task-person predictably respond? Obviously, he or she will say something like, "I'm busy," or "Come back later." The task-person tends to be so concerned about getting the job done that he or she doesn't care about socializing.

How will the people-person predictably respond? "Good to see you. It's a great time for a break. Let's talk." The people-person doesn't care nearly as much about getting the garden done as he or she does about developing relationships.

Mary and Martha are good examples of task- and people-oriented individuals. In Luke 10:40-41, Martha is task- or serving-oriented, while Mary is more interested in Jesus and her personal relationship to the Savior.

Martha was "cumbered about" with much service (Luke 10:40), while Mary was more interested in being near the Lord. It seems Martha was wrong, and Mary was right. In this case, we learn it is more important to be near Jesus than to serve Jesus.

73

But there are people who claim to be very spiritual and seldom accomplish tasks for God. If our worship does not translate into work, there is something wrong with our worship.

At the same time, we can work for Jesus and never get closer to Him. The reason this is true is because *whom* we serve and not *what* we serve is the most important principle we can learn. It is more important to know Him better, than to know what we should do for Him better. The Lord of the work is always more important that the work of the Lord!

In Colossians, Paul reminds us that "whatsoever ye do, do it heartily, as to the Lord, and not unto men" (3:23).

Another way of describing these differences is by using the terms "high-tech" and "high-touch." A high-tech approach is more concerned with process and thinking, while the person who uses a high-touch approach cares more about people and friendships. A high-tech person is into form and function along with the more how-to approach. A high-touch is more into feelings, caring, and sharing. A high-tech person is interested in things, while a high-touch person is concerned about people.

Some people are computer-smart but people-dumb. It is ironic that we can create a computer with artificial intelligence. It can think for itself, yet many of the inventors, computer geniuses of these modern advancements, cannot get along with their wives, children, or fellow employees.

NASA's Head of Mission Control

Once while I was conducting training in Houston near NASA, a gentleman came up to me after the seminar and asked if I would autograph a copy of my book *What Makes You Tick and What Ticks You Off*. The person behind him asked me if I knew who this man was. I realized he must be someone important.

He then introduced me to the Head of Mission Control at NASA. The man said I had fascinated him with my illustration of how rocket scientists could communicate with satellites millions of miles in outer space, but found it difficult to know how to communicate effectively with coworkers, who were just a few feet away. When we think of this example it is easy to see how people can be "computer-smart," but so "people-dumb." I also want to add the fact that we can be theologically "smart," while being people-dumb, or insensitive to the needs and emotions of others.

The sadder truth is that the more we develop and improve our machines, computers, and technology, which have no emotions, the less effective we are to those around us—our loved ones, our friends, and coworkers. This is why God wants us to learn and practice better people skills. We must not allow technology to become a substitute for our abilities to feel and care for others.

We need to remember that God cares for us and He wants us to do the same for others. I cannot overemphasize the importance of nurturing and improving all our relationships.

People can be a combination of active and passive, while task- or people-oriented.

There are many composites and blends of behaviors. Our personalities lean toward certain directions that guide our behavior in different situations.

Understanding our active/passive roles helps identify our specific temperament style. Combining these two different styles of influences with four specific character types can prove to be very enlightening. As we will see, some people are a mixture of both active/passive, while being both task/people-oriented at the same time.

Most people know if they are active extroverts or passive introverts. However, there can be confusion and frustration because not all extroverts are active toward people—others are active toward task accomplishments. In the same way, introverts can be passive in relation to people and/or tasks.

Understanding the four-quadrant model of basic human behavior sheds light on why this is so. It can make the difference between right and wrong responses, and help us discern the best or worst behavior in any situation.

DISC historical background

As stated earlier, Hippocrates, the father of modern medicine, first observed that there are four unique temperament types—four specific patterns of behavior. He thought it had something to do with the chemical makeup of the blood. He called these four types by their anglosized Greek names that translate to *choleric, sanguine, phlegmatic, and melancholy* to describe the four types.

Some years ago, as a young pastor I considered myself knowledgeable and wise in the area of temperament types. However, in reality I had not yet come to a point where I fully understood the practical aspects of the four temperaments. I had studied Tim LaHaye's excellent books on the subject in the 60s but had not fully learned the deeper lessons he was teaching concerning the temperaments.

After reading his book (which I wholeheartedly recommend), *The Spiritually Controlled Temperament*, I concluded that I was a choleric and God was also choleric! And that if you weren't a choleric, you needed to get right with the Lord. I thought everyone should be a choleric, if they were going to be dedicated to God.

The lesson I learned since then is that we are to be "all things to all people." You can be dedicated to God and not a choleric personality type. I also learned that I could be more Christlike when I'm an S- or C-type, even though that doesn't come easy for me. It may not be natural, but it can be supernatural.

In our next lesson, we're going to look at *Biblical Examples* of different personality types.

Biblical Examples

The Bible is full of unique personality types. Some individuals are aggressive and outgoing, while others are withdrawn and quiet. One type is not better than the other. Biblical behavior is balanced.

Scripture demands behavior from all corners of our chart. James 2:17 tells us that "faith without works is dead," while the prophet Isaiah in chapter 40 encourages us to "wait upon the Lord." Both verses deal with different behaviors, but are equally important.

Martha was more active and task-oriented, while her sister, Mary, was more passive and people-oriented. Martha demonstrated D-type behavior while Mary showed S behavior. (John 11:20)

When their brother Lazarus died, both Mary and Martha said the same thing to Jesus (John 11:21, 32), but Jesus responded differently to each one. The lesson is that we should respond to people according to *their* personalities—not ours. We should learn to emulate Christ. Don't be an intimidator or manipulator. Be an imitator of Christ!

If by any means I may provoke to jealousy those who are my flesh and save some of them. Romans 11:14

Biblical Examples

Individual **DISC** behavior is obvious in the Scriptures. Remember, God uses all types of personalities to complete His plan and purpose.

One of the most important lessons you can learn is that you don't have to let your personality type control you. Instead, allow God to control your personality and you will come out to be the winner every time!

It was an exciting new insight when I finally understood how the Holy Spirit wanted to also control my personality—the specific way that I think, feel, and act. He didn't want to just control my tongue, habits, and lifestyle. God wanted to also be the Lord of my personality. Let God control you with His Holy Spirit!

And do not be drunk with wine, in which is dissipation; but be filled with the Spirit. Ephesians 5:18

The following are examples of biblical characters that demonstrated specific personality types.

D-Types—

The apostle **Paul** was definitely a D-type. He was left for dead, imprisoned, stoned, forsaken, and forgotten. Yet he pressed on toward the high calling of God. He didn't worry about what anyone thought about him, except God. He also learned obedience and submission after God crushed him on the road to Damascus.

Sarah exhibited D behavior. She grew tired of waiting for God to give her the child He promised. So she dominated and devised her own way. She ordered Hagar to have a child. Sarah then raised the child as if he were her own. When she didn't like the way life turned out, she blamed Abraham. She also demanded Hagar to leave. She was dominant; however, her self-assurance and submissive behavior enabled her to leave her home for an undetermined destination. She knew it was the right thing to do.

I-Types—

Peter demonstrated I-type behavior every time he spoke up for the disciples. He was often very dramatic. One moment Peter promised in front of a crowd, to never forsake Christ; then a little later he denied the Lord, when no one is watching, to a young maiden. Yet God used Peter in a great way at Pentecost.

Ruth showed I behavior when she convinced Naomi to let her travel with her. Ruth demonstrated family loyalty and an adventurous spirit by her willingness to move to a foreign country. She was creative and industrious—so much so that she won the heart of Boaz, who was inspired and impressed by her work and loyalty. Ruth also was optimistic and influential in her pursuit of Boaz.

S-Types—

Moses seemed to show S behavior when God told him to lead the children of Israel out of Egypt. Moses was unsure of himself. He even tried to get Aaron to be the leader. Typically, S-type personalities don't like to be "up front"—telling everyone what to do—but God sometimes calls people to do great things in spite of their personality types.

Hannah is a good example of S behavior. She was submissive and remained faithful, even though her dreams were not fulfilled. She may have appeared "unstable" when she prayed in the temple. However, her reaction after praying shows she was very stable. She wanted the security that came with bearing children in her day. Hannah also wanted the support of her husband. She needed children to have an identity within her environment.

C-Types—

As a disciple, **Thomas** exhibited C behavior. This is especially evident when he doubted Christ's resurrection. C personalities need proof and answers to questions. Jesus didn't belittle Thomas but gave him the evidence needed to serve the Lord in a great way. Historians record that Thomas became an extremely effective missionary to India.

Esther seems to be a good example of C behavior. As the queen, she was willing to comply with the rules and requirements of her position. Yet when it became necessary to "bend" those rules, she wanted to make sure that it was done correctly. Esther prayed for reassurance and wisdom to proceed cautiously.

Regardless what specific temperament type you have, the most important lesson is to allow the Holy Spirit to control you. Don't let your feelings, thoughts, or natural motivations guide you. Instead, allow the Word of God and His Witness (the Holy Spirit) give you the direction you need.

In our next lesson, we're going to *Discover Your Behavioral Blends* and learn more about our composite personality types.

Discovering Your Behavioral Blends

Jewel

7

When you have two or three behavioral types evident in your composite personality, you're simply revealing that you can have more than one motivation influencing your actions, thoughts, and feelings. This could indicate that you have a healthy understanding of the uniqueness of your personality and that you know how to manage it.

Fifteen percent of people have only one primary DISC personality type. Eighty-five percent of people have a secondary type. In fact, most people have a blend or composite of behaviors, and they have a combination of two or more motivations.

You probably have a specific behavior blend—a combination of motivations that influences your feelings, thoughts, and actions. This, however, has nothing to do with Multiple Personality Syndrome. It simply means that people have normal combinations of influences, which affect the way they behave.

Behavioral blends *are not* like schizophrenia, either. There are normal combinations of personality types and there are abnormal types. Schizophrenia is caused by chemical imbalances and "short circuits" in the brain. The behavioral blends we are going to identify are normal and natural. Some are more prevalent than others, but all are evident in the lives of every normal believer in Christ.

Interestingly, after I conducted a seminar at the awesome Saddleback Community Church for Pastor Rick Warren, I had a lady call me to say she had been diagnosed with MPS (Multiple Personality Syndrome). She said she had four distinct personality types and that she just did my personality profile as each of her different personalities.

She was amazed to find that she had all four (DISC) personality types affecting her abnormal behavior. After she got off the phone, I told my wife, "That was easy: no matter what I told her, I was right!" I was taking liberties, joking about a very serious subject, but it seemed funny at the time.

Since then I have come to understand better the tremendous pain some people have with MPS. It is a serious problem and can't be written off as "craziness" or pure "demon possession." People with multiple personalities often have demonic influences, but I've found many, including some strong Christians, have clinically explainable problems.

Discovering that you have a behavior blend is not a clinical or abnormal situation. It is perfectly natural to have one, two, and even three DISC behavior types affecting why you do what you do.

Your Composite Behavior

To identify your behavioral blend, or composite behavior, find the definitions that best describe you.

As you do this, you will begin to understand your composite behavior. At the same time, you will learn how two or more types influence your personal motivations. This is not bad. It is not abnormal. It will simply explain how you may be affected by different feelings, thoughts, and desired actions at the same time.

Your behavioral blend not only affects how you relate to others, but how you relate to God and the Scriptures.

Discovering your giftedness should not only "wow" you but also challenge you. The Scriptures that admonish one person may not affect another person. The biblical references that speak to me may not mean as much to you. On the other hand, the Scriptures that challenge you may not affect me.

In other words, the Bible teaches everyone to be gentle. (1 Timothy 2:24) Certain personality types find gentleness easy, while gentleness is not as simple for another type.

Prayerfully consider the references that are listed with your behavioral blend pages. Controlling your behavior is easy as you yield to scriptural admonitions.

Review the following pages with your personality type in mind. See what lessons you can learn from studying your behavioral blend. Also study the other blends. Notice how there are many different composites of the four basic personality types.

Discovering Your Behavioral Blends

D:
DETERMINED DOERS

D-type individuals are dominant and demanding. They win at all costs. They do not care as much about what people think as they care about getting the job done. Their insensitivity to feelings makes them too strong. They are great at developing plans, but they need to improve their ability to do things correctly. Their strong will should be disciplined to prepare and think more accurately about what they are doing. They are motivated by serious challenges to accomplish tasks.

D/I:
DRIVING & DYNAMIC INFLUENCERS

D/I personality types are bottom line people. They are much like dynamic influencers. They are a little more determined and less inspirational, but they are strong doers and able to induce others to follow. They need to be more cautious and careful, as well as more steady and stable. They get involved in a lot of projects at the same time. They need to focus on one thing at a time and slow down. They are motivated by opportunities to accomplish great tasks through many people.

D/C or C/D:
DRIVING COMPETENT TYPES

D/C or C/D personality types are determined students or defiant critics. They want to be in charge, while collecting information to accomplish tasks. They care more about getting a job done and doing it right than what others think or feel. They drive themselves and others. They are dominant and caustic. Improving their people skills is important. They need to be more sensitive and understanding. They are motivated by choices and challenges to do well.

I:
INSPIRATIONAL INFLUENCERS

I personalities are impressive people. They are extremely active and energetic individuals. Approval is important to them. They can have lots of friends if they do not overdo their need for attention. They can be sensitive and emotional. They need to be more interested in others and willing to listen. They do not like research unless it makes them look good. They often do things to please the crowd. They are entertainers. They need to control their feelings and think more logically. They often outshine others and are motivated by recognition.

I/D:
INSPIRATIONAL DOERS

I/D personalities are super salespeople. They love large groups. They are impressive and can easily influence people to do things. They need a lot of recognition. They exaggerate and often talk too much. They jump into things without thinking them through. They need to be more studious and still. They should also be more careful and cautious. They are motivated by exciting opportunities to do difficult things. If not careful, they will do things to please the crowd and get themselves into trouble in the process. They make inspiring leaders and determined individuals.

I/S:
INSPIRATIONAL SPECIALISTS

I/S personalities are influential and stable. They love people and people love them. They like to please and serve others. They do not like time controls or difficult tasks. They want to look good and encourage others, but often lack organizational skills. They follow directions and do what they are told. They should be more concerned about what to do, than with whom to do it. They are motivated by interactive and sincere opportunities to help others. Regardless of being up front or behind the scenes, they influence and support others. They make good friends and obedient workers.

I/C or C/I:
INSPIRATIONAL COMPETENT

I/C and C/I types are inspiring, yet cautious. They size up situations and comply with the rules in order to look good. They are good at figuring out ways to do things better through a lot of people. They can be too persuasive and too concerned about winning. They are often impatient and critical. They need to be more sensitive to individual feelings. They are often more concerned about what others think. They do not like breaking the rules; neither do they enjoy taking risks. They need to try new things and sometimes go against the crowd. They are careful communicators who think things through.

S:
STEADY SPECIALISTS

S-type personalities are both stable and shy types. They do not like changes. They enjoy pleasing people and can consistently do the same job. Secure, nonthreatening surroundings are important to them. They make the best friends because they are so forgiving. Other people sometimes take advantage of them. They need to be stronger and learn how to say no to friends who want them to do wrong. Talking in front of large crowds is difficult for them. They are motivated by sincere opportunities to help others.

S/I:
STEADY INFLUENCERS

S/I personalities are sensitive and inspirational. They accept and represent others well. They have lots of friends because they are tolerant and forgiving. They do not hurt people's feelings and can be very influential. They need to be more task-oriented. They must learn to finish their work and do it well. They like to talk, but should pay more attention to instructions. They would be more influential if they were more aggressive and careful. They are kind and considerate. Motivated by opportunities to share and shine, they induce others to follow.

S/D and D/S:
STEADY DOERS

S/D and D/S combination types are the ones who get the job done. They prefer stable surroundings and are determined to accomplish tasks. As quiet leaders, they relate best to small groups. They do not like to talk in front of large crowds, but want to control them. They enjoy secure relationships, but often dominate them. They can be soft and hard at the same time. They are motivated by sincere challenges that allow them to systematically do great things. They prefer sure things, rather than shallow recognition. They make good friends, while driving to succeed.

S/C:
STEADY COMPETENT TYPES

S/C-types are stable and contemplative types. They like to search and discover the facts. They like to weigh the evidence and proceed slowly to a logical conclusion. They enjoy small groups of people. They do not like speaking in front of large crowds. They are systematic and sensitive to the needs of others, but can be critical and caustic. They are loyal friends, but can be too fault-finding. They need to improve their enthusiasm and optimism. They are motivated by kind and conscientious opportunities to slowly and correctly do things.

C:
CAUTIOUS COMPETENT TYPES

Those who have a C personality type are both logical and analytical. Their predominant drive is careful, calculating, compliant, and correct behavior. When frustrated, they can over do it or be the exact opposite. They need answers and opportunities to reach their potential. They tend not to care about the feelings of others. They can be critical and crabby. They prefer quality and reject phoniness in others. They are motivated by explanations and projects that stimulate their thinking.

C/S:
COMPETENT SPECIALISTS

C/S-types tend to always be right. They like to do one thing at a time and do it right the first time. Their steady and stable approach to things makes them sensitive. They tend to be reserved and cautious. They are consistent and careful, but seldom take risks or try new things. They do not like speaking to large crowds, but will work hard behind the scenes to help groups stay on track. They are motivated by opportunities to serve others and to do things correctly.

C/I/S, or I/S/C, or S/I/C:
COMPETENT INFLUENCING SPECIALISTS

People with the combination of C/I/S, I/S/C, or C/I/S like to do things correctly, impress others, and stabilize situations. They are not aggressive or pushy people. They enjoy large and small crowds, are good with others, and prefer quality. They are sensitive to what others think about them and their work. They need to be more determined and dominant. While they can do things well, they tend to be poor at making quick decisions. They are capable of doing great things through people, but need to be more self-motivated and assertive. They are stimulated by sincere, enthusiastic approval and logical explanations.

C/S/D, S/D/C, or D/C/S:
COMPETENT STEADY DOERS

C/S/D, S/D/C, or D/C/S are a combination of cautious, stable, and determined types. They are more task-oriented, but care about people on an individual basis. They don't like to speak in front of crowds. They prefer to get the job done and do it right through small groups, as opposed to large groups. They tend to be more serious. Often misunderstood by others as being insensitive, C/S/D, S/D/C, and D/C/S types really care for people. They just don't show it easily. They need to be more positive and enthusiastic. Natural achievers need to be friendlier and less critical.

I/D/S, D/S/I, and S/I/D:
INSPIRING DRIVING SUBMISSIVE TYPES

I/D/S, D/S/I, or S/I/D types can be impressing, demanding, and stabilizing at the same time. They are not as cautious and calculating as those with more C tendencies. They are more active than passive. But they also have sensitivity and steadiness. They may seem to be more people-oriented, but can be dominant and decisive in their task-orientation. They need to be more contemplative and conservative. Details don't seem as important as taking charge and working with people.

D/I/C, I/C/D, and C/D/I:
DOMINANT INSPIRING CAUTIOUS TYPES

D/I/C, I/C/D, and C/D/I personalities are demanding, impressing and competent. They tend to be more task-oriented, but can be people-oriented before crowds. They need to increase their sensitivity and softness. They don't mind change. Active and outgoing, they are also compliant and cautious. They like to do things correctly, while driving and influencing others to follow. Their verbal skills combine with their determination and competence to help them achieve their goals. Security is not as important as accomplishment and looking good.

STRAIGHT MIDLINE TYPES

(This behavioral blend can only be determined after you have completed your *Uniquely You Personality Profile* graph. Phone (706) 492-5490 to order a profile booklet or go to www.uyprofiler.com to complete your profile online.)

A straight midline blend occurs when all four plotting points are close together in the middle of the graph. This may indicate that the person is trying to please everyone. Striving to be *all things to all men* may indicate a mature response to pressure. Or it may confirm frustration over the intensity of differences under pressure. The person may be saying, "I really don't know what my D, I, S, or C behavior should be or really is." The person may want to do another profile after awhile to see if there is any change.

ABOVE MIDLINE TYPES

(This behavioral blend can only be determined after you have completed your *Uniquely You Personality Profile* graph. See note under Straight-Midline.)

Some patterns indicate unique struggles an individual may be having. An above midline blend occurs when all four plotting points are above the midline. This may indicate a strong desire to be overactive.

BELOW MIDLINE TYPES

(This behavioral blend can only be determined after you have completed your *Uniquely You Personality Profile* graph. See note under Straight-Midline.)

A below midline blend occurs when all four plotting points are below the midline. This may indicate that the person is not really sure how to respond to challenges. But God admonishes us to examine ourselves. "Let a man examine himself" (1 Corinthians 11:28a).

We should constantly examine ourselves in order to improve our effectiveness and relationships. It is always better to judge ourselves, rather than have someone else judge us. Even though judging others is wrong, people do it all the time.

If we would periodically take inventory of our behavior, as well as listen closely to those we love and those who love us about how we tend to respond, especially under pressure, we would be much better off.

There are often several factors and influences that affect us. Therefore, understanding our behavioral blends can help us correct and improve our actions and reactions.

Controlling Your Behavioral Blend

The bottom line is allowing the Holy Spirit to control your personality. People often say, "I just want to be me." They want to find themselves and be "real." The problem is that when you really find yourself, you often don't like what you find. You might be so dictatorial, self-seeking, insecure, or critical that God seems powerless in your life.

The so-called "real" or "natural" you can be the opposite of what God wants you to be. You should not seek to be normal, but spiritual; not natural, but supernatural—to do what you do through the power of God in your life, to be what God wants you to be through a personal relationship with Him by faith in Jesus Christ as your Savior and Lord. (Ephesians 2:8-10)

Be conformed into the image of Christ!

It wasn't until I began to understand my strengths and uniqueness in light of the controlling power of the Holy Spirit that my personality changes (or perhaps, better said, "personality controls") began to take place in my life.

When I was the pastor of a growing church in Florida, one of my dear friends, an elder, came to me one day and said, "Mels, the servant of the Lord must not strive, but be gentle." My first thought (with an attitude) was, "What, do you think I am not gentle?!" I wanted to correct him and show my strong displeasure with his counsel. Who was he to tell me I was not gentle?

About a month or so later, another good friend and leader in the church came to me and said, "Mels, the fruit of the spirit is gentleness!" I thought, "Conspiracy! They're ganging up on me!" But because I knew these two men loved and respected me, I trusted that God might be using them to help me, though it still hadn't sunk in yet.

Finally, a little later a third friend (I felt like Job by this time) came to me and said, "Mels, you're too strong and forceful at times." I thought, "That does it! They've all gotten together to attack me." But the Holy Spirit began to really work on me.

Around this time I had taken a summer course at Dallas Theological Seminary with Dr. Frank Wichern, the staff psychologist, and learned about the DISC Model of Human Behavior. I already knew about the choleric, sanguine, phlegmatic, and melancholy types, but had never heard about the four DISC-types.

I pursued my studies under Dr. John Geier, Chairman of the Human Behavior Science Department at the University of Minnesota, and had become certified to teach his Personal Profile System. The more I taught it, the more God used it to help me learn about myself.

I finally decided to create my own DISC profile from a biblical perspective and spent many, many hours praying and researching how to make my profile practical and powerful for God's glory.

I didn't want another academic exercise or a simple "feel good about yourself" assessment. I wanted something that would change lives and empower Christians to serve the Lord better. The following insights with specific biblical references came out of days and months of searching for Scriptures that might apply specifically for each behavioral blend.

D:
DETERMINED DOERS

• Be careful to not offend when you take charge—"The servant of
      the Lord must not strive [be pushy], but be gentle"
(2 Timothy 2:24). Anger is normal, but must be controlled—"Be
      angry and sin not" (Ephesians 4:26).
• Be motivated to purity and peace—"Wisdom from above is first
      pure, peaceable" (James 3:17).
• Focus on doing ONE thing well—"This ONE thing I do"
      (Philippians 3:13, emphasis added).
• Always remember, God is the master of your fate—"The fear of
      the Lord is the beginning of wisdom" (Proverbs 1:7).

D/I:
DRIVING & DYNAMIC INFLUENCERS

• Though naturally fearless and able, you need to respect God's
      power over you—"Fear God and give Him glory"
      (Revelation 14:7).
• Guard the overuse of strength and be kind—"By the meekness
      and gentleness of Christ" (2 Corinthians 10:1).
• Making peace is a greater challenge than winning a fight—
      "Blessed are the peacemakers" (Matthew 5:9).
• Choose words carefully—"A soft answer turns away wrath"
      (Proverbs 15:1).
• God must control your feelings—"The fruit of the Spirit is . . .
      temperance [self-control]" (Galatians 5:23).

D/C:
DRIVING COMPETENT TYPES

• Seek to get along with everyone—"Live peaceably with all men" (Romans 12:18).
• Be kind and loving—"Kindly affectionate one to another" (Romans 12:10).
• Show more love—"Love one another" (1 John 4:7).
• Seek to serve, not to be served—Be a "servant of Christ" (Ephesians 6:6).
• Meekness is not weakness. Control your desire to have power over others. Be Christlike—"By the meekness and gentleness of Christ" (2 Corinthians 10:1).
• Take time to be still and commune with God—"Be still and know that I am God" (Psalm 46:10).

I:
INSPIRATIONAL INFLUENCERS

• Don't exalt yourself—"Humble yourself and God will exalt you" (James 4:10).
• Be sure to listen more—Be "quick to hear, slow to speak" (James 1:19).
• Work at being organized—"Do all things decently and in order" (1 Corinthians 14:40).
• Concentrate on doing what is most important—"All things are not expedient" (1 Corinthians 10:23).
• Prepare more—"Prepare yourself" (2 Chronicles 35:4).
• Be careful what you desire—"Delight in the Lord" (Proverbs 3:5-6).

• Don't be overconfident and watch what you promise—Peter claimed he would never deny Christ. (Mark 14:31)

I/D:
INSPIRATIONAL DOERS

• Guard the power of your words—"The tongue is a fire" (James 3:6).
• Don't be like those who "by fair words and good speeches— deceive" (Romans 16:18).
• Always tell the truth—"Speak the truth and lie not" (1 Timothy 2:7).
• Remember who has blessed you—"God must increase, I must decrease" (John 3:30).
• Give God the glory for all you do—"Give unto the Lord glory" (Psalm 29:1-2).
• Put God first in your life—"Seek ye first the kingdom of God" (Matthew 6:33).
• Beware of the "lust of the flesh and pride of life." They will ultimately destroy your talents. (1 John 2:16)

I/S:
INSPIRATIONAL SPECIALISTS

• Do everything unto the Lord—"Whatsoever you do, do it heartily, as unto the Lord and not unto men" (Colossians 3:23).
• Beware of seeking man's approval—"Not with eye service as men pleasers" (Ephesians 6:6).

- Seek to please God, rather than others—"Do always those things that please Him" (John 8:29).
- Be more task-oriented—"Sit down first and count the cost" (Luke 14:28).
- Don't be lazy—Do "not [be] slothful in business" (Romans 12:11).
- Work hard—"Let every man prove his work" (Galatians 6:4).
- Don't just talk about what you want—"Being fruitful in every good work." (Colossians 1:10).
- Be industrious—"Night comes when no one will work" (John 9:4).

I/C:
INSPIRATIONAL COMPETENT TYPES

- Be careful not to think too highly of yourself—"God resists the proud, but gives grace to the humble" (1 Peter 5:5).
- Seek to please God more than others—It is best "when a man's ways please the Lord" (Proverbs 16:7).
- Be a good example—"Be an example of the believer" (1 Timothy 4:12).
- Care more about how you look to God—"Glorify God in your body and spirit" (1 Corinthians 6:20).
- Be bold and confident in Christ—"We have boldness and access with confidence by the faith in Him" (Ephesians 3:12).
- Guard statements and judgments—"A lying tongue is a vanity tossed to and fro" (Proverbs 21:6).
- Don't flatter yourself—"He flatters himself in his own eyes" (Psalm 36:2).

S:
STEADY SPECIALISTS

- Increase your confidence in Christ—"I can do all things through Christ, Who strengthens me" (Philippians 4:13).
- God is your "rock, fortress and deliverer" (Psalm 18:2).
- Fearfulness is not from God—"God has not given you the spirit of fear" (2 Timothy 1:7).
- Speak out more often—"Let the redeemed of the Lord say so" (Psalm 107:2).
- Be more outgoing and less inhibited—"Christ has made us free" (Galatians 5:1).
- Be more assertive—Moses confronted Pharaoh with "Let my people go" (Exodus 5:1).
- Security is possible—"You are secure, because of hope" (Job 11:18).

S/I:
STEADY INFLUENCERS

- Speak out—Be "bold to speak without fear" (Philippians 1:14).
- Take stands—"Stand fast in one spirit" (Philippians 4:1).
- The Spirit of God can help you tell others about Christ—"The Spirit of the Lord is upon me" (Isaiah 61:1).
- Guard against fearfulness—"Let not your heart be troubled, neither let it be afraid" (Luke 14:27).
- Remember, you don't need "people" to encourage you— "David encouraged himself in the Lord" (1 Samuel 30:6).
- Always do right and don't fear people—The "fear of man brings a snare [trap]" (Psalm 29:25).

S/D and D/S:
STEADY DOERS

- God wants to empower what you think is weakness—"Most
  gladly will I rather glory in my infirmities that the power of
  Christ may rest upon me." (2 Corinthians 12:9).
- God's grace (the power and ability to do what God wants) is
  enough for whatever you need—"My grace is sufficient"
  (2 Corinthians 12:9).
- You are often strongest in weakness, as you trust in God and not
  yourself—"For when I am weak, then am I strong"
  (2 Corinthians 12:9).
- Encourage and help others daily—"Exhort one another daily"
  (Hebrews 3:13).
- God challenges you to reason with Him—"Come now and let us
  reason together" (Isaiah 1:18).

S/C:
STEADY COMPETENT TYPES

- Be assertive and stronger—"only be strong and very
  courageous" (Joshua 1:6).
- Be more enthusiastic—"Whatever you do, do it heartily"
  (Colossians 3:23).
- Enjoy relationships, rather than endure them—Christ said, "I am
  come that you might have life . . . abundantly"
  (John 10:10).

• Peace and happiness do not come from security and safety—
"Peace I leave with you, my peace I give unto you"
(John 14:27).
• Divine peace is knowing God's ways are beyond ours—"The
peace of God passes all understanding" (Philippians 4:7).
• Be fearless in Christ—"I will fear no evil" (Psalm 23:4).

C:
CAUTIOUS COMPETENT TYPES

• Be more patient when wanting to correct others—"Rebuke,
exhort with all longsuffering," 2 Timothy 4:2.
• Correct in love—"Speak the truth in love" (Ephesians 4:15).
• Be more positive—"Rejoice in the Lord always"
(Philippians 4:4).
• Hope in God, not circumstances—"Rejoicing in hope"
(Romans 12:12).
• The most logical thing you can do is serve God—"Present your
bodies a living sacrifice . . . which is your reasonable
service" (Romans 12:2).
• Find happiness in God—"Delight in the Lord" (Psalm 37:4).

C/S:
COMPETENT SPECIALISTS

- Think more positively—"Whatsoever things are pure . . . of good report . . . think on those things" (Philippians 4:8-9).
- Guard against the fear of failure—God promises "Fear not for I am with you" (Isaiah 43:5).
- Focus on the possible—"With God all things are possible" (Matthew 19:26).
- Be cheerful—"The fruit of the Spirit is . . . joy" (Galatians 5:22).
- When everything goes wrong, God is all you need—"Our sufficiency is of God" (2 Corinthians 3:5).
- Think like Christ—"Let this mind be in you which was also in Christ" (Philippians 4:8).

C/I/S, I/S/C, and S/C/I:
COMPETENT INFLUENCING SPECIALISTS

- Guard against being judgmental—"Judge not lest you be judged" (Matthew 7:1). "Who are you that judges another?" (James 4:12).
- Avoid bitterness and resentment—"Lest any root of bitterness spring up to trouble you" (Hebrews 12:15).
- God will meet your needs—"My God shall supply all your need according to His riches in glory" (Philippians 4:19).
- Be thankful for everything—"In all things give thanks" (1 Thessalonians 5:18).
- Let God's Word affect you—"Let the Word of God dwell in you richly in all wisdom" (Colossians 3:16).

• Whatever you do, do it for God's glory—"Do all in the name of God" (Colossians 3:17).

C/S/D, S/D/C, and D/C/S:
COMPETENT STEADY DOERS

• Be more enthusiastic—"Whatever you do, do it heartily as unto the Lord" (Colossians 3:23).
• Don't worry so much about problems—"Let not your heart be troubled" John 14:27.
• Be more positive —"Whatsoever things are pure . . . if there be any virtue, think on these things" (Philippians 4:8-9).
• Let your sensitivity be more evident—"Be kindly affectionate, one to another" (Romans 12:10).
• Don't be like Moses when he was reluctant to lead because of his poor verbal skills (Exodus 4:10-16).
• Be more outwardly optimistic and encouraging to others— "Exhort one another daily" (Hebrews 3:13).

I/D/S, D/S/I, and S/I/D:
INSPIRING DRIVING SUBMITTING TYPES

• Be more calculating and careful—"Sit down first and count the cost" (Luke 14:28).
• Organize yourself and attempt to be more organized—"Do all things decently and in order" (1 Corinthians 14:40).
• Be careful what you promise—"Let your 'yea' be 'yea' and your 'nay' be 'nay'" (2 Corinthians 1:17).

- Give God the glory for all you do—"Give unto the Lord glory" (Psalm 29:1-2).
- Think before you do things—"A wise man thinks to know" (Ecclesiastes 8:17).
- Be humble and share the glory—"Humble yourself and God will exalt you" (James 4:10).

D/I/C, I/C/D, and C/D/I: DOMINANT INSPIRING CAUTIOUS TYPES

- Be sure to listen more—Be "quick to hear, slow to speak" (James 1:19).
- Be more sensitive to the individual's feelings—"The servant of the Lord must not strive, but be gentle" (2 Timothy 2:24).
- Be more of a peacemaker—"Blessed are the peacemakers" (Matthew 5:9).
- Be more steady and don't get sidetracked—"Be steadfast, always doing the work of the Lord" (1 Corinthians 15:58).
- Don't be judgmental—"If a man be overtaken in a fault, restore him" (Galatians 6:1).

STRAIGHT MIDLINE TYPES

(This behavioral blend can only be determined after you have completed your *Uniquely You Personality Profile* graph. Phone (706) 492-5490 to order a profile booklet or go to www.uyprofiler.com to complete your profile online.)

- You may be trying to be "all things to all men," which is good, but it can be frustrating at times.

• Recognize your identity in Christ—"I am crucified with Christ, nevertheless I live, yet not I, but Christ lives in me" (Galatians 2:20).
• Relax in the Lord—"Come unto me all you that labor and are heavy laden and I will give you rest" (Matthew 11:28).
• You cannot please everyone all the time—"Having men's persons in admiration" (Jude 16).

ABOVE MIDLINE TYPES

(This behavioral blend can only be determined after you have completed your *Uniquely You Personality Profile* graph. See note under Straight Midline.)

An above midline blend may be trying to overachieve—"It is God who works in us, both to will and do of His good pleasure" (Philippians 2:13). You may be thinking too highly of what is expected of you. Remember Peter!

BELOW MIDLINE TYPES

(This behavioral blend can only be determined after you have completed your *Uniquely You Personality Profile* graph. See note under Straight Midline.)

A below midline blend may indicate you are not really sure how to respond to challenges—"I can do all things through Christ" (Philippians 4:13).

• Think more positively about yourself—"I am fearfully and wonderfully made" (Psalm 139:14).

C-types are often overly cautious and doubtful. Be careful that your personality doesn't control your analytical thinking. Be open and honest. If in doubt, ask a friend if the description is like you or not.)

"Search me, O God, and know my heart: try me, and know my thoughts" (Psalm 139:23).

This information regarding the control of your behavioral blend is perhaps the most important in this entire book. Unless we learn how to let the powerful Word of God dwell and rule in us richly, we will never be all that God wants us to be.

My Personal Experience

I remember, as if it were yesterday, when I was in Tulsa, Oklahoma, at an anti-Communist conference in 1973 and Dr. Jack Hyles, the late pastor of the First Baptist Church of Hammond, Indiana, was speaking on the filling power of the Holy Spirit.

I had heard so many preachers emphasize the "anointing of God," but often thought it was something mystical and emotional. One night after the meeting I decided I wasn't going to bed until I knew that I was "filled by the Spirit."

I remember so well walking the streets of downtown Tulsa asking God to show me that I was filled with the Spirit. I looked for a sign. I waited for a feeling. I sought some kind of miracle proof. Finally, in the early morning hours, God reminded me of His Holy Word—Ephesians 5:13, "Don't be drunk with wine, wherein is excess, but be filled with the Spirit." I realized the key was to be controlled by His will and way: the control of His Spirit is what the "filling" was all about.

Just like alcohol causes us to do things we wouldn't

ordinarily do, so the Holy Spirit wants to control us to do things we wouldn't ordinarily do. When we are filled or controlled by God's Spirit, then we will pray even though we don't feel like praying. We will witness even when, in the flesh, we don't want to witness. We will study the Word, even when we, in the flesh, don't want to study the Word.

For the first time in my Christian life (I had been in full-time Christian work for over seven years), I came to understand that the filling of the Holy Spirit was simply "obedience to God" and allowing Him to do His work through me.

I began to understand what it meant to be "crucified with Christ" and that the life I was to live was His life in me. (Galatians 2:20) It was a liberating day to discover that the filling (controlling) power of the Spirit was not a feeling or a miraculous experience, but rather a way of life—an obedience of moment-by-moment yielding to His control over my thoughts, feelings, and actions.

I now realize this encompasses my giftedness, my spiritual gifts, personality type, passions, and all that make up the me in Christ. Once you have identified your behavioral blends, you can now begin to understand how your specific spiritual gifts relate to your personality type, as well as how God wants to bless and benefit you for His glory.

Combining Natural

(your personality type)

and Supernatural

(your spiritual gift type)

Motivations

Jewel 8

Combining spiritual gifts with personality types is a modern concept. When I first began thinking about how spiritual gifts and temperaments may relate, there was nothing to confirm or even encourage my suspicions. To the best of my knowledge, no one had written or researched the possibility.

Ray Stedman encouraged identifying our spiritual gifts for the purpose of serving one another in the church back in the 60s. Dr. John Geier from the University of Minnesota designed the first DISC personality profile in 1977, but no one had put them together.

As a theologian, I recognized from the Scriptures how spiritual gifts were our supernatural motivations. I also came to understand how personality types were our natural motivations. Human behavior science was fascinating to me. I had the opportunity to study under Dr. Geier, and in 1984 I was certified as a Human Behavior Consultant. I thought I should keep the spiritual and scientific separate. I constantly wondered if these two motivations in our lives could be combined to get a complete picture of why we do what we do.

I remember conducting a seminar for Dr. Charles Stanley at the First Baptist Church of Atlanta in 1992. I focused on identifying our DISC personality types. That night I mentioned how I never met a "sweet, soft, and sensitive" (S-type) personality with the gift of prophecy. Or how there was no such thing as a "dominant, direct, and demanding" (D-type) personality with the gift of showing mercy. These combinations were very opposite types and I thought were impossible combinations. This became a night I'll never forget!

After the seminar, a gentleman came to me and said he had the gift of prophecy and had just discovered he had an S-type personality. I said to myself, "You must have done the profile wrong!" I kindly told him his situation was very unusual and that I would research his combination of a spiritual gift with a personality type that did not seem to suit it.

Not long after, a young lady went through my training who was a nurse. She discovered at my seminar she had a D-type personality. She already knew she had the gift of showing mercy, and I wondered how it could be combined with a "direct and demanding" (D) personality type.

These dichotomies and oxymorons were extremely confusing. I thought, God is a God of harmony and only gives spiritual gifts that relate to our personality types. So why would believers have gifts that didn't seem to relate to specific personality types?

I really struggled with this concept. I couldn't find anyone who had researched or even mentioned it in their teachings. I spent an entire day at the Dallas Theological Seminary library searching for information that might help me. I even met with one of the most respected professors at the seminary to ask what he thought. He had concluded that God gives spiritual gifts that relate to our natural personality types. The idea of combining our natural and supernatural motivations seemed foreign to him.

After much further study I have concluded that, though it is rare and uncommon, relationship of two opposite motivations in one person does occur. God is not in a box. He does what He pleases. That's why we emphasize the "Uniquely You" in Christ.

After profiling and interviewing thousands of Christians, I have found that there are certain spiritual gifts that combine most often with specific personality types. I have also discovered that every spiritual gift can be combined with each personality type. Some combinations are much more common than others, but every combination is possible, because "it is He who has made us."

D- and C-type personalities often have the gifts of prophecy or administration/ruling. "Exhorters" are often I- or S-types. The gift of teaching corresponds best to C behavior.

Sometimes God combines a specific personality with an unrelated spiritual gift.

I used to say, "I never met a prophet with an S-type personality." After much prayer and study, I noticed Jeremiah was the "weeping prophet," (Jeremiah 3:21). He perceived and proclaimed truth but was also sensitive. God does unique things with our motivations.

Nay but, O man, who art thou that replies against God? Shall the thing formed say to him that formed it, Why hast thou made me thus? Isaiah 29:16; 45.9

115

God does what He pleases. The Lord sometimes gifts individuals with seemingly opposing endowments and enablements—differing natural and supernatural giftedness. It's not common, but it is normal. It will also explain why some Christians are often confused and frustrated by their conflicting motivations.

People with the gift of prophecy are often serious and hard on those who are indifferent to right and wrong. The gift of prophecy comes across with more D- and C-type behavior. But S-type prophets can be very sensitive and stable. They are motivated by a strong sense of loyalty to and protection of those they love.

Most people have spiritual gifts that relate to their personality types. But regardless of whether your spiritual gifts and personality type relate to each other, God has a purpose for gifting you the way He has. Be open to the unique way God wants to use you.

Recognizing your uniqueness can help you find your place of service. As previously stated, everybody is somebody in His body. Scripture is full of admonitions that encourage you to get involved in the ministries of your church.

Discovering your giftedness helps you understand how God has designed you to glorify Himself.

Whether therefore ye eat, or drink, or whatsoever ye do, do all to the glory of God 1 Corinthians 10:3

Identifying your unique combination can be liberating. Some believers have uncommon (not abnormal) combinations. Unfortunately, most Bible teachers today describe spiritual gifts in temperament terms. For example, the gift of showing mercy is always described in S terms—sensitive, sweet, and soft, but there are those with the gift of showing mercy and a D-type personality. They demand that everyone shows mercy!

The following definitions of spiritual gifts combined with the DISC personality types are simple insights. As you examine yourself and those around you, you will see God's wonderful design in action. Read each definition for maximum insights.

Study the following pages with your combination profile in mind. Notice how each personality type affects each spiritual gift.

D & I with Administration/Ruling

D-Type with the Gift of Administration/Ruling

Demanding-type Christians with the gift of administration are strong leaders. They like to tell others what to do. They often see what needs to be done and delegate the work to others. They can be too bossy. D-Administrators tend to see the big picture, but lack warmth to get others to help without pressure. They can intimidate and offend if not careful. Often concerned more about tasks than people, they need to be more sensitive and loving. D-Administrators can be gifted leaders who press forward to do great things for God.

I-Type with the Gift of Administration/Ruling

Influencing-type Christians with the gift of administration are optimistic leaders. Their positive enthusiasm encourages others to get involved. They can be overly excited. They tend to talk people into doing things they don't want to do. They impress others with their friendliness and verbal skills. I-Administrators need to guard against manipulating. They should serve by example. They often take on more than they can handle, disappointing those who expect a lot from them. However, they can accomplish much through people.

S & C with Administration/Ruling

S-Type with the Gift of Administration/Ruling

Submissive-type Christians with the gift of administration are concerned about getting tasks done in steady and stable ways. They need to be more assertive and aggressive. S-Administrators can be too sacrificing. They are faithful in whatever they do, but need to inspire others to help. They can be quiet leaders, challenging others by example. They tend to be shy. Sometimes, they surprise others with their serious concern to accomplish tasks. S-Administrators are achievers who like to work through small groups.

C-Type with the Gift of Administration/Ruling

Cautious-type Christians with the gift of administration are competent taskmasters. They recognize needs and organize others to meet those needs. They enjoy doing things completely right the first time. They tend to be picky. They can increase effectiveness with more warmth and team participation. Working through people and creating an enthusiastic atmosphere can be helpful. They should avoid being critical of what others do. C-Administrators are best able to get groups to do the right things.

119

D & I with Apostleship/Pioneering

D-Type with the Gift of Apostleship/Pioneering

Christians who are driven to start new churches often have the gift of apostleship. They like impossible challenges.

D-type apostles today are determined and demanding. They don't let obstacles get in their way. They plod on through the thick and thin of birthing something from nothing. They are decisive and determined to organize new ministries, especially among different cultural and ethnic groups. They are active, task-oriented individuals who demonstrate tremendous confidence and authority.

I-Type with the Gift of Apostleship/Pioneering

Christians who constantly use their influence and enthusiasm to start new churches often have the gift of apostleship. They tend to be very inspiring and energetic about reaching other groups, especially those of other cultures. Those with I-type personalities and the gift of apostleship are active, people-oriented individuals. They tend to step out into uncharted regions and groups in order to start new ministries. They make great impressions while using their authority, but should guard their excitement.

S & C with Apostleship/Pioneering

S-Type with the Gift of Apostleship/Pioneering

Steady and stable type Christians who are uncharacteristically passionate about starting new ministries may have the gift of apostleship. They are slow and shy, but determined about their ideas. They are consistent and don't give up easily. They don't have to always be up front, but are compassionate and sensitive about reaching out to other groups. Those with S-type personalities with the gift of apostleship have a quiet but strong vision and authority about starting new churches.

C-Type with the Gift of Apostleship/Pioneering

Typically cautious and calculating Christians who are committed to starting new churches often have the gift of apostleship. They tend to be overly careful and research things to death. But their plans and programs are just what new churches need. They don't mind standing alone. They are passive, task-oriented individuals. They are stimulated by the need for organization. They enjoy putting people and programs together in order to start new ministries, often to different types of cultures and groups.

D & I with Craftsmanship

D-Type with the Gift of Craftsmanship

Active/task-oriented personalities with the gift of craftsmanship are dominant, direct, and demanding. They tend to be pushy and bossy about the job at hand. They are more risk taking and often take on the most difficult challenges. They need to be in control. They focus on completing the task regardless of what others think or feel. They are decisive doers, taking charge and getting the job done. Their gift of craftsmanship makes them specialists, while their personality makes them very industrious.

I-Type with the Gift of Craftsmanship

Active/people-oriented personalities with the gift of craftsmanship are very personal and friendly. They love to use their gift to inspire and influence others. They tend to be more expressive than others. They use their creativity and ability to make things with their hands to encourage others. They love to talk about what they do. They work best in groups. Their gift of craftsmanship motivates them to do things with their hands, while their I-type personalities relate well with people.

S & C with Craftsmanship

S-Type with the Gift of Craftsmanship

Passive/people-oriented personalities with the gift of craftsmanship are sensitive, supportive, and specialists. They are motivated to serve others through their gift of craftsmanship. They make the most loyal and faithful workers. They don't need a lot of recognition or approval. They tend to not like crowds and work best in small groups. Their gift of craftsmanship makes them very capable at whatever they do, while their S-type personality makes them concerned about each individual's needs.

C-Type with the Gift of Craftsmanship

Passive/task-oriented personalities with the gift of craftsmanship tend to be the most cautious and competent when it comes to whatever they do. They are critical thinkers and workers and want to do things right the first time. They tend to be picky perfectionists and not people-oriented and friendly. They also are more interested in doing things well. Their concern about quality and correctness helps to make them excellent craftsman, yet they need to improve their people skills.

D & I with Creative Communication

D-Type with the Gift of Creative Communication

D-type personalities with the gift of creative communication are driven and determined to use drama for God's glory. They love to present powerful performances that communicate biblical truth. As active/task-oriented personalities, they use their creativity to communicate lessons that impact and change lives. They tend to be very aggressive and assertive. Every drama is a serious production. They often need to control themselves more than others. Demanding and dedicated, they often work too hard. They are industrious and committed to communicating the lesson in creative ways. They also work tirelessly at getting the job done.

I-Type with the Gift of Creative Communication

These are the perfect combination of personality and the spiritual gift of creative communication. The I-type personality is very inspiring and influencing, while the gift of creative communication is imaginative and expressive. They have high egos and can be easily hurt if not approved or recognized for their talent. Those with I-type personalities and the gift of creative communication must always remember God made them to shine for His glory, not theirs. They also should be willing and ready to praise others, rather than seek praise for themselves. They are the most suitable for drama presentations, but must discipline their time to prepare more.

S & C with Creative Communication

S-Type with the Gift of Creative Communication

More shy than outwardly expressive, they will often surprise you with their passionate presentations. Privately, they are quiet and reserved, but in front of a crowd, those with the S-type personalities and the gift of creative communication come alive and seem out of character. They serve best as part of a team or small group. They don't seek to be "the star." They sacrificially give of themselves to please others, while communicating biblical truth in a creative way. They may be more comfortable serving behind the scenes as support staff. Whatever their role, they are faithful servants committed to creatively communicate messages of love and hope.

C-Type with the Gift of Creative Communication

When it comes to designing and presenting dramas, no combination of personality and spiritual gift will do it in as organized a way as C-type personalities with the gift of creative communication. They are calculating and competent specialists that communicate truth in the most creative ways. They tend to be moody melancholies and need to lighten up while rehearsing and presenting. They tend to be too serious. Their people skills are often lacking, but they seem to overcome this shortcoming with their ingenious and creative ways of doing the tasks so well. This is reflected in the fact that they are great at planning and perfecting presentations that communicate a message.

D & I with Discernment

D-Type with the Gift of Discernment

Active/task-oriented Christians with unusual discernment about right and wrong are D-type personalities with the gift of discernment. They tend to be pushy and controlling with their discernment. They have great insights, but often use them in a demanding and driving way. They enjoy using their discernment to confront or challenge others to obey God's Word. They need to be more sensitive and compassionate concerning what they feel is a particular problem.

I-Type with the Gift of Discernment

Christians who constantly inspire and influence others through their discernment of right and wrong are often I-type personalities with the gift of discernment. They seem to flaunt their discernment and sometimes come across as boastful. Those who use their intuitive senses to encourage and lift up others often have active/people-oriented personalities. They make a great impact on people. They are enthusiastic and get really excited when they can use what they discern about things to help others.

S & C with Discernment

S-Type with the Gift of Discernment

The more passive/people-oriented Christians with great intuition often have S-type personalities with the gift of discernment. They are not pushy or controlling. They are often very quiet and wait for opportunities to share what they discern about a problem. They especially love to share how the Word of God applies to a particular situation. However, they are often very shy. They don't like to make others uncomfortable, and can be tremendous friends and sources of encouragement and direction.

C-Type with the Gift of Discernment

Compliant and calculating types with unusual intuition often have C-type personalities with the gift of discernment. They tend to be picky and often "too right" for most people to appreciate, but they make the greatest resource when it comes to making practical decisions. This combination is best at choosing the right direction, but needs to be more sensitive to how their discernment might affect others. With more inspiring and optimistic attitudes, this combination is powerful and respected.

D & I with Encouragement

D-Type with the Gift of Encouragement

Decisive-type Christians with the gift of encouraging are persistent encouragers. They tend to dominate conversations with practical steps-of-action. They like to share advice. D-Exhorters are driven to control the situation in order to encourage. They need to be more flexible and sensitive. People can't always do or feel what D-Exhorters want. They tend to have a plan for every problem. Often impatient, they can be too pushy. Letting others share their ideas, while remaining determined to encourage others, makes them extremely effective.

I-Type with the Gift of Encouragement

Inspiring-type Christians with the gift of encouraging make enthusiastic encouragers. They impress others with their advice, but they can be too optimistic. They often create high expectations. They need to be more realistic. I-Exhorters should guard against using their verbal skills to manipulate others. They may try to influence others to do more than humanly possible. They should listen more and speak less. Interested in others, they often induce positive responses. I-Exhorters communicate encouragement best.

S & C with Encouragement

S-Type with the Gift of Encouragement

Sensitive-type Christians with the gift of encouraging are sweet encouragers. They share simple and slow steps of action to help others. They often wait for others to ask for advice and are not pushy. They love to stabilize bad situations with practical ideas. S-Exhorters also can be too shy. They may wait instead of aggressively confronting an issue, which proves that they need to be more assertive. However, their concern for others often makes them too accommodating. The truth remains that they may need to show "tough love." S-Exhorters are security-oriented encouragers.

C-Type with the Gift of Encouragement

Calculating-type Christians with the gift of encouraging are precise encouragers. They often know just what to say. Their practical plans of action tend to be concise. They make competent counselors with specific insights, but they can be too hard on people. C-Exhorters can see what needs to be done, but fail at communicating love. They should be more sensitive to the failures of others. Having patience and kindness will increase effectiveness. They should not be so critical. C-Exhorters make great problem-solvers.

D & I with Evangelism

D-Type with the Gift of Evangelism

Dynamic and demanding type Christians with the gift of evangelism can be extremely effective. They are self-starters with a sense of urgency, but their driving concern to win souls can make them too pushy. D-Evangelists should be more gentle and patient. Determined to get the job done, they often feel like everyone should be involved in evangelism. Direct with their presentations, they like sermons that explain the gospel and offer invitations to trust Christ. D-Evangelists are dedicated to "making Him known."

I-Type with the Gift of Evangelism

Influencing-type Christians with the gift of evangelism are most enthusiastic about soul winning. Their enthusiasm is also very contagious—they are cheerleaders for Christ. Interested in people, they are "natural born" witnesses. I-Evangelists make sharing the gospel look so easy. Because of their strong desire to impress, they may care as much about what people think of them as they do about leading others to Christ. They must constantly remember God gave them gifts to shine for Him, not self. I-Evangelists can win many souls to Christ.

S & C with Evangelism

S-Type with the Gift of Evangelism

Sweet and soft type Christians with the gift of evangelism are gentle witnesses. They steadily share the gospel. They don't like to force issues. They tend to be too nice. Scoffers often waste S-Evangelists' time. Knowing they will go the extra mile, some people take advantage of them. Avoiding confrontation, these stable types prefer "friendship evangelism." But their motivation to win souls often overcomes their natural reluctance to speak out. S-Evangelists enjoy bringing people to Jesus without a lot of fanfare.

C-Type with the Gift of Evangelism

Cautious and compliant type Christians with the gift of evangelism are the most thorough witnesses. They like to go point-by-point, convincing people to understand every detail. They try to have an answer for every question, but they can overwhelm others with too many facts. C-Evangelists are often more concerned with the task, rather than the person in need. As competent individuals, they need to be more flexible and friendly. C-Evangelists can turn doubt into a fascinating opportunity for Christ.

D & I with Faith

D-Type with the Gift of Faith

Active/task-oriented Christians who constantly demonstrate an unusual amount of dependence upon God often have the gift of faith. They tend to be more demanding than most people. But they also often challenge others to have more faith. They are stimulated by the Word of God to increase their faith. They are very driven and decisive. They don't take a long time to make up their minds. They like to move forward in faith once the decision has been made. They tend to have great faith when things look hopeless.

I-Type with the Gift of Faith

Christians who get most excited about believing God often have the gift of faith. They are extremely enthusiastic and inspire others to increase their faith. They are very expressive and talk a lot about the joy of trusting the Lord for everything. I-type personalities with the gift of faith are sometimes too optimistic and rush in where angels fear to tread. They need to be more cautious and guard their faith from making miscalculated decisions, but they make great encouragers in difficult times.

S & C with Faith

S-Type with the Gift of Faith

Passive/people-oriented Christians who seem to trust God when everyone else has given up often have the gift of faith. They are more quiet and shy, but have an internal source of strength. S-type Christians with the gift of faith are not expressive or loud about their faith. They have a steadiness and stability that makes them highly respected and sought out when it comes to increasing a group's faith. They are not pushy or bossy, but are firm and strong when it comes to believing God's Word.

C-Type with the Gift of Faith

This is a unique combination because of the differences between the C personality, which is one of cautiousness and concern, and the person who has the gift of faith who is motivated to trust God regardless of the cost. C-type personalities with the gift of faith have a dichotomy of being able to trust God while researching all the options. They prefer more information before making their final decisions, but have an unusual amount of faith, even when all the facts are not clear. They prefer in-depth research, but stand strong on the promises of God.

D & I with Giving

D-Type with the Gift of Giving

Domineering-type Christians with the gift of giving are serious about financial matters. They can be very successful in business. They also have the "gift of getting." They tend to use money to control others. Demanding how finances are used, they can be extremely picky with budgets. They seldom give to the wheel that squeaks the loudest. When it comes to financial decisions, they are either unbending or influencing. However, they will either discourage or encourage others with their money and/or advice. When all is said and done, they make great financial counselors.

I-Type with the Gift of Giving

Impressing-type Christians with the gift of giving are enthusiastic about stewardship. They like to encourage everyone to be givers because they make great promoters. However, they can kill projects because their persuasive abilities and financial concerns. I-Givers are more optimistic than others. In reality, they can be too positive. Their faith is evident in giving, but can become prideful. They like to tell everyone how to give more. When discouraged, they may use their verbal skills and financial credibility to influence others. I-Givers are most excited when a situation involves finances.

S & C with Giving

S-Type with the Gift of Giving

Security-oriented type Christians with the gift of giving are not risk takers. They are submissive (willing) givers. They may lack the vision necessary to take on challenging projects. Sensitive to individual needs, they help others behind the scenes. They are private about giving. S-Givers can be too helpful. They need to govern their sincere desires to serve with a stronger determination to do what is right. Because they tend to be the most sacrificing, if they are not careful, others may take advantage of them. S-Givers are stable financial planners who avoid financial disasters.

C-Type with the Gift of Giving

Compliant-type Christians with the gift of giving are cautious. They move conservatively. They seldom make quick financial decisions. They don't like pressure. Vision and growth are often stifled because of pessimism. C-Givers seldom make investment mistakes, but may miss great opportunities. They need to be more positive. People often think they are critical. They should be more friendly. Respected by others, they should use their competence to help, rather than find fault. They can be valuable in financial planning.

D & I with Healing

D-Type with the Gift of Healing

Driven and determined, D-type personalities with the gift of healing are extremely passionate about seeing people delivered from sickness and disease. They are very aggressive and strong about God's power to heal. They don't take no for an answer. They tend to be so unwavering and demanding that some people find them offensive and too pushy. D-type personalities with the gift of healing need to be more sensitive to those who are not as responsive or optimistic. They have tremendous faith but need to remember that it's not their faith that heals.

I-Type with the Gift of Healing

When it comes to believing God for healing, those who have inspiring and impressive personalities with the gift of healing tend to be the most emotional and expressive. These people are very dramatic and often may be too "theatrical." Therefore, they need to guard their enthusiasm. They are obviously on fire for the Lord, but must be careful they don't turn their zeal for healing into wildfire and confusion. They should seek to always be controlled by the Spirit, rather than the flesh. They have a weakness toward making things overly exciting and seeking attention, but are the most influencing when others need healing.

S & C with Healing

S-Type with the Gift of Healing

Reserved and quiet, S-type personalities with the gift of healing tend to be more sensitive and patient. When it comes to believing God will heal, they are not pushy but are serious. They are faithful and consistent in their prayers for healing and tend to be more humble and sincere. S-type personalities with the gift of healing are often not as aggressive as others, but they are just as firm and committed to healing. They are silent witnesses, always willing and ready to serve when needed. They are not very bold or expressive, but are steady and stable believers in God's healing.

C-Type with the Gift of Healing

C personalities who have the divine gift of healing tend to be more passive and task-oriented. They are very studious and cautious and don't tend to be as loud or excited as others, but they can be just as serious. Sometimes they tend to be too concerned. They need to improve their people skills and be more friendly. They love to research and explain why God heals today. They tend to be very knowledgeable. They can be naturally cautious, but biblically optimistic about God's power to heal. They are a unique blend of a compliant personality with a supernatural faith.

D & I with Hospitality

D-Type with the Gift of Hospitality

Christians who are demanding, but always volunteer their homes for meetings or for those needing a place to stay, truly may have the gift of hospitality. They are active/task-oriented individuals who are driven and determined to make their homes a blessing for others. When it comes to hospitality, they tend to be controlling but also may find that others take advantage of them. They love to plan meetings and entertain people in their homes. However, make no mistake about it, they are ones who will be in charge.

I-Type with the Gift of Hospitality

Enthusiastic and excited Christians who love to invite others to their homes often have the gift of hospitality. They are "social butterflies." They love to entertain and welcome people in their homes. I-type personalities with the gift of hospitality openly and often express their interest in having groups or individuals over any time or for any reason. They need to be more organized and plan better. This combination can be very difficult on other family members, but their gracious hospitality is always encouraging to those who visit with them.

S & C with Hospitality

S-Type with the Gift of Hospitality

Christians who are more quiet and shy, but always ready and willing to have groups or individuals in their homes, often have the gift of hospitality. They may not seem expressive or outgoing, but they are optimistic about the opportunity to help others through opening their homes. S-type personalities with the gift of hospitality often sacrifice themselves for the sake of making others feel comfortable in their homes. They have real servants' hearts, and may often have trouble saying no to others.

C-Type with the Gift of Hospitality

Cautious and calculating type Christians who love to open their homes to others often have the gift of hospitality. They tend to have neat homes and impress others with their cleanliness. C-type Christians with the gift of hospitality like to have all the details worked out before opening their homes. They love to entertain others, even at the last minute, but always want it to be done in an orderly way. They are thinkers and analyzers—passive/task-oriented individuals who love to have others in their homes.

D & I with Intercession

D-Type with the Gift of Intercession

Determined-type Christians with the gift of intercession seem driven to pray for others. Understandability, they take prayer seriously. They also believe everyone should improve his or her prayer life and this can lead them to appear to be a little pushy and dominant. However, when the Holy Spirit controls them, they are tireless prayer warriors. They have a strong faith that God answers prayers if we will simply petition Him faithfully. They need to be more understanding of those who are not as concerned about prayer as they. They can be confrontational about prayer, but their commitment to intercessory prayer is their greatest strength.

I-Type with the Gift of Intercession

Inspiring and influencing personalities who are serious about intercession tend to be very excited and enthusiastic about God answering prayer. They are expressive and love to talk. They are committed to prayer and can pray long, heartfelt petitions. They love to share how God answered specific prayers and are extremely optimistic and encouraging. For balance, they need to be more quiet and humble about their gift. They also should allow others to talk more while they listen better. However, they make tremendous prayer partners and friends.

S & C with Intercession

S-Type with the Gift of Intercession

Passive/people-oriented personalities with the gift of intercession are very reserved and more interested in small group or individual prayer times. They are faithful friends to the end. They don't like to get in front of large crowds, but can be counted on to pray privately. They don't need a lot of enthusiasm or excitement to pray. They consistently intercede on behalf of those who are hurting and need special prayer. They ought to be more assertive in challenging others to pray more. But when it comes to needing someone you can count on, they are the most faithful intercessors.

C-Type with the Gift of Intercession

Cautious and calculating Christians who are committed to prayer tend to be C-type personalities with the gift of intercession. They are more competent and compliant about prayer. They go by the book and do everything decently and in order. They don't tend to be very sociable or outgoing. They need to be more expressive and friendly. They don't mind being by themselves, interceding in prayer for others. They are more analytical and systematic about their prayer lives. For them, intercessory prayer is a serious task that demands their time, place, and devotion.

D & I with Interpretation

D-Type with the Gift of Interpretation

Active/task-oriented Christians with the gift of interpretation are able to translate what others speak in unknown languages. They tend to be control-oriented and like to take charge and make things happen. They don't like to wait until someone does something. They often speak out and are the first to interpret what is being spoken in tongues. They need to be more sensitive to people's feelings. They tend to be hard and strong with others. They are very decisive and sure of what they are doing. Their interpretations are often direct and demanding. They make confident translators and interpreters of what is spoken in tongues.

I-Type with the Gift of Interpretation

Expressive/people-oriented Christians with the gift of interpretation are very inspiring when they translate what others speak in tongues. They are more enthusiastic and obvious as they stand out and speak up. They usually don't wait to be asked to translate. They tend to be more emotional than others. They love to be seen and heard. They need to be more humble about their divine gift. I-type personalities with the gift of interpretation should always remember God made them to shine for His glory, not their glory. They often encourage others through their impressive translation of what is being spoken in unknown languages.

S & C with Interpretation

S-Type with the Gift of Interpretation

Sweet and sensitive personalities with the gift of interpretation tend to be more passive. They are not very aggressive or assertive. They tend to be stable and security-oriented when translating inspired speech. They are soft spoken and don't like to force themselves or their interpretations on others. They seem to be more loving and caring than most people, but they can be taken advantage of when others see them as weak. They need to learn to be more confident and bold. They are quiet servants, ready to help others by interpreting what is being spoken in tongues.

C-Type with the Gift of Interpretation

Passive/task-oriented personalities with the gift of interpretation tend to be very precise and exact. They don't like confusion. Instead, they like to make things clear. They tend to be overly analytical. They may take a simple interpretation of what someone is speaking in tongues and turn it into a long explanation. As a result of this, they can seem to be too critical and hard on others. They tend to be very compliant and want everything done correctly. C-type personalities with the gift of interpretation are focused on translating inspired speech with accuracy. They don't like shallow messages. They would rather interpret deep messages that are logical and clear.

D & I with Knowledge

D-Type with the Gift of Knowledge

Christians who are decisive and direct, with quick answers to a wide range of questions, often have the gift of knowledge. They don't hesitate to share what they know from the Bible and other subjects. They are confident and demanding. D-type personalities with the gift of knowledge are more active/task-oriented with what they know. They tend to be more results-oriented, using their knowledge to accomplish tasks and move toward fulfilling a goal or a difficult challenge.

I-Type with the Gift of Knowledge

Inspiring and impressive type Christians who have a lot of knowledge of the Bible and other subjects often have the gift of knowledge. They tend to be very expressive—sometimes they talk too much. They tend to have a Scripture verse and answer for everything. I-type personalities often talk a lot, but those with the gift of knowledge seem to have unusual knowledge over and above most other people. They are very upbeat and encouraging with their information.

S & C with Knowledge

S-Type with the Gift of Knowledge

Sweet, soft, and sensitive type believers who seem to have an unusual amount of information about so many things often have the gift of knowledge. They are slow to share but, when asked, have an answer for just about everything. They are more shy than outgoing. Usually, they don't volunteer their knowledge, but are ready once asked. S-type personalities with the gift of knowledge are faithful and loyal. They don't like hurting others and want to always help others with their knowledge.

C-Type with the Gift of Knowledge

Christians who tend to be very careful and compliant, but exhibit tremendous Bible knowledge and are informative about various other subjects, often have C-type personalities with the gift of knowledge. They love to research and understand why things are so. They love to use their knowledge of the Bible to explain things. They tend to be a little too deep for most people, but are a great resource. They often need to lighten up and learn how to be more people-oriented.

D & I with Leadership

D-Type with the Gift of Leadership

Active/task-oriented Christians who like to take charge and direct groups to accomplish difficult tasks often have D-type personalities with the gift of leadership. They don't take no for an answer. They tend to plan and push forward, challenging others to follow. They don't like sitting still and waiting for things to happen. They like to make things happen and tend to motivate and mobilize people for accomplishing the task at hand. They like long-range planning with specific short-term goals that involve lots of people moving forward together.

I-Type with the Gift of Leadership

Christians with a lot of energy and enthusiasm, who constantly rise to the top in leading others, often have I-type personalities with the gift of leadership. They love to impress and inspire others to follow. They are not confrontational. Instead, they use their tremendous people skills to create exciting climates for growth. They love to be up front and have great verbal skills. They struggle between responding to what people think of them and moving forward. They often come across as proud or egotistical, but are best at leading groups with their optimistic attitudes.

S & C with Leadership

S-Type with the Gift of Leadership

Christians who seem to be shy, but demonstrate tremendous abilities in influencing others to follow, often have S-type personalities with the gift of leadership. Their S/servant-type behavior seems unlikely to challenge others to follow, but they make tremendous "quiet leaders." They tend to be soft spoken and easy going. They don't like to offend anyone and work hard at keeping everyone happy. Their sensitive leadership skills cause them to be very effective at getting groups to move out in unity.

C-Type with the Gift of Leadership

Calculating and critical thinking type Christians, who demonstrate the unusual ability to motivate others, often have C-type personalities with the gift of leadership. They go by the book, doing a lot of research and being careful to not do anything wrong. Their influence on followers is often more cautious and conservative. They don't make quick or careless decisions. They plan their work and work their plan to get others involved in moving ahead. Their leadership style is more analytical and organized.

D & I with Mercy

D-Type with the Gift of Mercy

Determined-type Christians with the gift of mercy are rare, but are dedicated to helping others feel better. When confronting misery, they go into action by getting others involved and giving them direction on how to help the hurting. Their domineering ways tend to conflict with their desire to sympathize with others. They can be decisive, while at the same time being merciful and kind. D/mercy-types are unique individuals who tend to demand that everyone display a caring spirit. Their driving personalities can be misunderstood as insensitive, while mercy is their motivation. They press the need to care. They should guard their dominance with loving hearts.

I-Type with the Gift of Mercy

Inspiring-type Christians with the gift of mercy influence others to care more. They use verbal skills to generate excitement for the cause of demonstrating love. Interested in people, they induce strong feelings of concern. They also can be very emotional. I/mercy-types can overdo their influence. Some people may think their concern is all show. They like to impress others with their kindness. They need to calm down and be more humble. When it comes to evident sensitivity, I/mercy-types are tops. They provide cheer to those suffering.

S & C with Mercy

S-Type with the Gift of Mercy

Sensitive-type Christians with the gift of mercy are most loving. They are sweet servants always ready to help. They specialize in responding to times of suffering. S/mercy-types may be so concerned that they miss opportunities to teach lessons. They can also be fooled by insincere cries for help. They may need to be more assertive with those who use their pain as an excuse. They should be more demanding. They may need to share truth, rather than always listening. When people hurt, S/mercy-types shine.

C-Type with the Gift of Mercy

Compliant-type Christians with the gift of mercy are extremely concerned about others. They see needs no one else sees. They tend to know exactly what to say. They are careful not to miss opportunities to help, but can be critical of those who don't get involved. C/mercy-types may try to analyze why people hurt. Their conservative care is often appreciated. They need to be optimistic. Enthusiasm and inspiration are often lacking. C/mercy-types are competent individuals who care about the sufferings of others.

D & I with Miracles

D-Type with the Gift of Miracles

Active/task-oriented personalities with the gift of miracles are driven and determined to see God work supernaturally. They are very optimistic. They strongly believe nothing is impossible and often try to impose their faith on others. They need to be more patient and kind. They also tend to be pushy and bossy. God has enabled them to perform supernatural acts to authenticate specific messages or ministries. Their strong personalities often make them very powerful leaders. They need to always remember that they have no power apart from God.

I-Type with the Gift of Miracles

Active/people-oriented personalities with the gift of miracles are very expressive and seek to perform supernatural acts. They tend to be extremely excited and enthusiastic whenever God uses them to do miracles. They are passionate about seeing God work through them in miraculous ways. They tend to have high egos and can become proud of their gift. They need to remember that God only allows them to reflect His glory. They are mirrors of God's grace and power. They should guard against "showmanship." They are the most exciting supernatural servants.

S & C with Miracles

S-Type with the Gift of Miracles

Passive/people-oriented personalities with the gift of miracles are soft-spoken, but powerful when it comes to God working miracles through them. They seem to be the most unlikely tools for God to use, but have tremendous faith in the supernatural acts of God. They tend to be too reserved. They can surprise you with their quiet demeanor and divine power to authenticate messages or ministries through the working of miracles. They are humble and kind servants. They especially want to help behind the scenes. They don't seek praise, but should accept it for God's glory.

C-Type with the Gift of Miracles

Passive/task-oriented personalities with the gift of miracles are more meticulous and detail-oriented. They want to do one thing at a time and do it right the first time. They want to understand everything, but perform supernatural miracles that cannot be explained. They are more analytical and cautious. They are not flippant or silly. They are very serious, especially when it comes to seeing God do the impossible. Their personality and spiritual gift don't seem to mesh. But they are tremendous testimonies of how God works supernatural miracles through them, in spite of their natural doubts.

D & I with Pastor/Shepherd

D-Type with the Gift of Pastor/Shepherd

Demanding-type Christians with the gift of pastor/ shepherd tend to be ministry driven. Seeing the big picture, they are compelled to lead others. Their domineering ways can be misunderstood as dictatorial. They may be genuinely dedicated to shepherding others, but have strong feelings about the way things should be done. Slowly working through people will make them more effective. Often taking charge, they seem to control others. Their concern for the flock is evident. D-Pastor/Shepherds make great visionaries.

I-Type with the Gift of Pastor/Shepherd

Inspiring-type Christians with the gift of pastor/shepherd are impressive. Their influence makes people enjoy working and worshiping. They can be extremely successful and must guard against pride. People look up to I-Pastor/Shepherds. Able to persuade, they need to be more cautious of what they promote. They love to minister and encourage others to do so. Often concerned too much about what others think, they need to guard against using people to build their ministries. They can be best at using their ministry to build people up.

S & C with Pastor/Shepherd

S-Type with the Gift of Pastor/Shepherd

Submissive-type Christians with the gift of pastor/shepherd are selfless servants. They enjoy building relationships that result in effective ministries. They shepherd by example, not demand. The problem that can arise is that they can be too nice. Often more caring than confrontational, they may need to be more assertive. Concerned about the ministry, they should be more enthusiastic. Shyness often hinders their leadership. People appreciate their interest in ministry, but some may want them to be more decisive. S-Pastor/Shepherds make gentle leaders.

C-Type with the Gift of Pastor/Shepherd

Conscientious-type Christians with the gift of pastor/shepherd are methodical. They like to go by the book. They don't like to take risks and venture away from what they know works. They may need to be more open to innovation. They strive for correctness. Purity in the group is important to C-Pastor/Shepherds. Their enthusiasm will encourage more to minister. Often conservative, they tend to be picky. Detailed assignments for everyone can often be overdone. C-Pastor/Shepherds are competent church leaders.

D & I with Prophecy/Perceiving/Proclaiming

D-Type with Gift of Prophecy/Perceiving/Proclaiming

Demanding-type Christians with the gift of prophecy are fearless concerning truth. Determined to preserve purity, they tend to dominate others. As protectors of righteousness, they proclaim truth without concern for what anyone thinks. They often feel like they have the divine right to be pushy. D-Prophets are so driving, they often offend others. They need to be more gentle, rather than always striving to expose error. They should be more sensitive to the feelings of others. D-Prophets are the most effective declarers of truth.

I-Type with Gift of Prophecy/Perceiving/Proclaiming

Influencing-type Christians with the gift of prophecy make great communicators of truth. They articulate correctness with persuasion. They tend to over use enthusiasm and emotions to convince others. Able to induce action or reaction, they need to guard against verbal abuse. Proclaiming truth, I-Prophets should season their speech with sugar. Making great impressions, they must remember who they represent, not what they defend. I-Prophets are inspiring protectors of the faith.

S & C with Prophecy/Perceiving/Proclaiming

S-Type with Gift of Prophecy/Perceiving/Proclaiming

Sensitive-type Christians with the gift of prophecy are shy, but serious about truth. While they seem to be soft, their sense of concern makes them persuaders. Motivated to proclaim truth, they tend to be gentle, but strong. S-Prophets struggle with their concern for individuals versus their desire to stand for correctness. This balance makes them surprisingly effective. People are often impressed when their shyness turns into firmness. They need to be careful about extremes. When it comes to truth, S-Prophets are like sleeping giants.

C-Type with Gift of Prophecy/Perceiving/Proclaiming

Calculating-type Christians with the gift of prophecy are both cautious and competent. They tend to be conscientious, but they also can be too critical of those who, in their view, compromise truth. Often convincing, they tend to be confrontational. Their concern for compliance often makes them unbending. C-Prophets are insightful, but can be insensitive to what others feel. They should increase effectiveness with greater interest in others, rather than always insisting on being right. As protectors of truth, C-Prophets are able to see and share correctness.

D & I with Serving/Ministry/Helps

D-Type with the Gift of Serving/Ministry/Helps

Driving-type Christians with the gift of serving/ministry/ helps stay busy for Christ. They tend to work hard behind the scenes, doing whatever needs to be done. They can be impatient with those who don't help. Determined to minister, they tend to dominate and intimidate others to also serve. D-Servants are task-oriented individuals who seem to work tirelessly. They may need to slow down, relax, and delegate. They can become demanding and offensive. D-Servants are dedicated to ministering and helping others. They are self-sacrificing doers of the Word.

I-Type with the Gift of Serving/Ministry/Helps

Inspiring-type Christians with the gift of serving/ministry/ helps are excited about serving. Their impressive enthusiasm makes others want to get involved. They can be too persuasive and impatient. I-Servants are extremely effective in inducing action. They tend to oversell and manipulate. Influencing others, they should guard their verbal skills when the job needs to get done. I-Servants tend to work longer than necessary, because they talk too much. Creating an exciting atmosphere of service is their specialty.

S & C with Serving/Ministry/Helps

S-Type with the Gift of Serving/Ministry/Helps

Steady-type Christians with the gift of serving/ministry/helps are every church's dream—they are the backbone of ministry. If anything needs to get done, they faithfully serve without recognition. They are not bossy, but should be assertive. People can take advantage of S-Servants. They should be more aggressive in seeking help. Being always sensitive to the feelings of others makes them sought out. However, sometimes they solve problems for those who may need to feel the pressure of their irresponsibility. S-Servants are the most stable servants.

C-Type with the Gift of Serving/Ministry/Helps

Competent-type Christians with the gift of serving/ministry/helps are detail-oriented. They don't like loose ends. If anything needs to be done right, they are perfect for the job but tend to be difficult to work with. They can be too picky. They need to be friendlier and cooperative. Often feeling like they are the only ones who ever do anything, they need to appreciate others more. Positive attitudes and enthusiasm are recommended but difficult for C-Servants. They can be the hardest working and most compliant servants.

D & I with Teaching

D-Type with the Gift of Teaching

Demanding-type Christians with the gift of teaching are dedicated students and energetic instructors. They like challenging research in order to convince others. They tend to be too forceful. D-Teachers make strong disciplinarians. Often domineering, they need to learn how to be more gentle with their insights. Digging deep without getting to the point can be frustrating. They should balance dedication to teaching with more people-orientation. When it comes to explaining why something is true, D-Teachers get the job done.

I-Type with the Gift of Teaching

Inspiring-type Christians with the gift of teaching are most interesting. They tell the best stories. They use clear illustrations. Their verbal skills create fascinating studies, but their classes can be lengthy. I-Teachers need to be more time-conscious. They may also stretch the text to make a point. Concerned about what others think, they often make good impressions. They can become prideful because of their tremendous ability to communicate. I-Teachers are some of the most interesting instructors.

S & C with Teaching

S-Type with the Gift of Teaching

Stable-type Christians with the gift of teaching are systematic researchers. They like to teach steadily, step-by-step. Their simple but insightful instruction often lacks excitement. They need to be more animated. S-Teachers are faithful, loyal friends, who tend to resist conflict. They should strive to be more interested in results than in relationships and revelation. Concerned about harmony and accuracy, they can be too sweet and slow to share why something is true. You can count on S-Teachers for thorough explanations.

C-Type with the Gift of Teaching

Compliant-type Christians with the gift of teaching are controlled by the quest for truth. They make great researchers. Determined to discover in-depth truth, they can overdo their lessons. They can become too factual. People seem to find C-Teachers competent but boring. They also can lack enthusiasm and warmth. Therefore, they should focus more on practical applications. As critical thinkers, C-Teachers can sound sarcastic. When sensitive, excited, and patient, C-Teachers make great instructors

D & I with Tongues

D-Type with the Gift of Tongues

Dominant and driving type personalities with the gift of tongues are very strong and aggressive. They speak with authority and power but tend to be too serious and commanding. They need to be more sensitive and understanding. D-type personalities with the gift of tongues are confident that God speaks through them in unknown languages. They often call for commitments. They are confident and convincing leaders. Their messages tend to be forceful. They need to be more soft and caring about other people's feelings as they speak God's Word in tongues.

I-Type with the Gift of Tongues

Influencing and impressive type personalities with the gift of tongues tend to be the most emotional. They are very exciting and enthusiastic. They can overreact and become hysterical. They need to do things decently and in order. They are great communicators, but sometimes people think they speak in tongues too long or too loud. Others often wonder how real or sincere I-type personalities with the gift of tongues are. They need to be more humble and learn to listen better. They have tremendous verbal skills that make their speaking in tongues very inspiring.

S & C with Tongues

S-Type with the Gift of Tongues

Naturally shy personalities with the gift of tongues are unique Christians. They tend to be shy, yet their speaking in tongues publicly is a powerful testimony of God's control. They prefer to speak in heavenly languages privately, in their own closets. S-type personalities with the gift of tongues are more quiet and reserved. They tend to be soft-spoken, but while speaking in tongues, they seem to be out of character. This powerful blend is very supportive and affecting. They are steady and stability-oriented. They don't like change but will speak out in tongues.

C-Type with the Gift of Tongues

Naturally passive and cautious type personalities with the gift of tongues tend to be conscientious and more reserved than others. Speaking in unknown languages is unusual for C-types, who are more skeptical and critical-thinking than most. Their messages tend to be more in-depth and boring. They need to work on being more enthusiastic and less scholarly. They don't like confusion. Instead, they prefer to speak in tongues so that people can understand serious messages. Being spontaneous is unnatural for them, but their supernatural speaking in tongues is also unusual and powerful.

D & I with Wisdom

D-Type with the Gift of Wisdom

Active/task-oriented Christians who demonstrate unusually good judgment often have D-type personalities with the gift of wisdom. They tend to be more direct and demanding with their wisdom. They often openly challenge others if they believe a decision is unwise. They have a great respect and trust in the Word of God. They need to be more loving and kind, but their decision-making is often very accurate. They tend to be more confronting, not waiting for people to come to them. They make great counselors when people want straightforward and honest answers.

I-Type with the Gift of Wisdom

Christians who get very excited about sharing their insights and concerns about right and wrong often have I-type personalities with the gift of wisdom. They tend to be very expressive, talk a lot, and often demonstrate extremely good judgment. Unlike other I-type personalities, who tend to talk a lot about nothing, those with the gift of wisdom show great depth of thought. However, they need to guard their verbal skills and learn to listen more. When they do share, their wisdom is often surprising and insightful. They have a unique combination of articulating wisdom without sounding foolish.

S & C with Wisdom

S-Type with the Gift of Wisdom

Passive/people-oriented Christians with the unusual ability to make wise decisions often have S-type personalities with the gift of wisdom. They are not hard and strong about most things, but when it comes to right and wrong, they do have unique insights. They are often sought out by others because of their loyal and faithful way of dealing with problems. They are quieter than most people, but when they do share their wisdom, people are often amazed. They tend to be humble and need to speak out more. But they often demonstrate wisdom that few people ever imagine.

C-Type with the Gift of Wisdom

Cautious and slow decision-makers, who also have great judgment, are often C-type personalities with the gift of wisdom. They tend to be extremely analytical and sensitive to right and wrong. They are not very outgoing or expressive. They prefer to research and dig into the Bible in order to discover in-depth truth. They share their wealth of wisdom in detail with those who ask. They don't tend to volunteer their wisdom and often come across as uncaring. They should increase their enthusiasm and interest in people. They often have a lot of wisdom, but little "personality."

Once you have identified your primary and secondary spiritual gifts, along with your specific personality type, study all the blends to better understand how other people tend to think, feel, and act as combination types. This will help you recognize how you and others may have unusual and uncommon blends of behavior.

Begin praying about how God can use you according to your giftedness. In our next lesson, we're going to look at *Where Does Your Giftedness Fit Best in Ministry?*

Where Does Your Giftedness Fit Best in Ministry?

God gifted you to glorify Himself. He also blesses you for honoring Him. The Greek word for gift is *charis*. Its meaning is related to the emotion of joy. In other words, God's plan is to bless you with "joy unspeakable" through your natural and spiritual motivations. He created you to experience joy in your life.

Pastor Peter Lord used a tremendous illustration about a lawn mower stored in a garage and never being used to cut the grass. If that lawn mower had a heart, it would be very sad, because it was made to cut grass. Staying in a garage is not what a lawn mower is meant to do.

Imagine if someone took the lawn mower out of the garage and began to cut the grass. The lawn mower would be so excited. You could hear it say, "Wow! This is what I was meant to do—cut grass!"

As believers, we were created to know God and make Him known. We also were made to glorify Him and to serve Him as Lord. We will never be happier than when we fulfill this eternal purpose. However, many Christians are miserable because they don't understand how God wants to exercise His gifts through them.

They have never learned that true enjoyment only comes when we let God's grace guide our lives. His grace is not only "undeserved favor," it also is the motivating force that gives us the ability and power to do God's will. Each one of us has been given a measure of God's grace in order to glorify Him. He has designed each one of us to honor and serve Him. We do this best when we allow Him to use our giftedness in ministry. Jesus reminded his disciples, "If any man serve me, him will my father honor" (John 12:26).

Scripture also admonishes us "to obey and serve [the Lord]." When we do this, we will spend our "days in prosperity, and [our] years in pleasures" (Job 36:11).

Typically, God uses people in specific areas based upon their giftedness. However, He also uses all personalities and spiritual gifts in great ways. As we have discussed earlier, no personality or spiritual gift is better than another. God uses all of us to accomplish His will in His timing.

Sometimes God even uses our personalities in special ways that are contrary to and beyond our giftedness.

Moses is the best example of how God can use a person with S-type behavior to be a great leader. God also used the apostle John, who was called the "son of thunder," to write three epistles of love, joy, and fellowship (1, 2, & 3 John). However, this same apostle who wrote the gospel of John and the book of Revelation seems to portray a D-type personality, which is one of strength and power. His "son of thunder" personality is evident, but his gentle and sweet emphasis in the epistles is obviously more S-type in character.

John also felt so comfortable in the Lord's presence that he laid his head on Christ's chest—an act that is more like a son in relationship to a father. He also showed great compassion by willingly taking care of the Lord's mother, Mary, at the Crucifixion. John is a great example of balance—high-tech and high-touch—active and passive for God's glory.

We also see how God used Luke to pen the gospel of Luke and the book of Acts in great detail. As a physician, Luke demonstrated C-type behavior through the careful research of his writings. Jeremiah, though a strong prophet, showed great emotion and God used this as motivation in his life. His prophecies continue to bring conviction, hope, and direction for our lives today.

In fact, each one of these men and countless others—men and women—have been used by the Lord. It is not their natural, human abilities that stand out; it is their giftedness in Christ that makes the difference in this sin-darkened world.

The Church is in desperate need of volunteers and servants to help with the work of the ministry. God never intended the paid staff to do all the work. In Ephesians 4:11-12 we see how the Lord is in the process of training God-gifted leaders to be equippers— people who do not do all the work themselves. It only makes sense that churches need people who are ready and willing to be equipped for God's work!

Remember, in God's eyes, every member is a minister!

Another truth that we must face is the fact that we all want to be served. However, God has called us to serve one another. Ministers, staff, and church members are all to serve Christ together—each with their functions and giftedness.

The primary job of the pastor and staff is to equip and train members to do the work of the ministry in their church. Lay leaders can serve as counselors, teachers, leaders, helpers, and in many other roles. Churches are greatly blessed when members share in the responsibility of church ministry, and they grow in proportion to the number of people who get involved.

The sad truth, however, is that far too many churches are paralyzed by the lack of member involvement. Ministers and staff are overworked and underpaid, while church members fail to get involved in the ministry of the church.

The happiest and healthiest churches are those where most of their members consider themselves as ministers. The strongest and most effective churches have tremendous volunteer staffs. Everyone is blessed. Involved members are especially blessed, because God honors them. The result is happy and healthy churches.

Once you identify your giftedness, getting involved can be extremely enjoyable. You will feel comfortable and confident when you serve where you fit best. You will also be more effective since you will operate out of your strengths. The question is:

Where do you fit best?

Identifying your profile does not measure maturity or calling. It may suggest that you can teach well. However, you may be a new Christian and need to grow and learn more about the

Bible before you attempt teaching others. The apostle Paul had to wait and mature for three years after he came to love the Lord before God began to use him in a great way.

If this is the case in your life, don't be discouraged! There are many ministries that you can do within the church. You can function as a teacher's assistant, class secretary, or organizer of class socials. Be faithful in the little things and God will give you a chance to be faithful in the bigger opportunities later. Problems arise when new Christians, especially D- and I- type personalities, want to take charge or be up front without growing to a place of maturity and humility. They need to serve for God's glory and not for self.

Recognizing involvement from a giftedness perspective is vital to our effectiveness.

Involvement from a Spiritual Gifts Perspective

One of the best ways to grow as a Christian is to get involved. Identifying your natural and spiritual motivation will help. Many believers desire personal growth, but seldom find a rewarding ministry.

The following is a summary of spiritual gifts and how they can impact your life.

ADMINISTRATION/RULING

Abilities: Organizing or delegating tasks.
Opportunities: Group leader and office personnel.
Warning: Avoid thinking everyone will get involved.
Reward: Seeing people work together to accomplish difficult tasks.
Prayer: Dear God, help me to be tolerant of those who don't respond as I think they should.

APOSTLESHIP/PIONEERING

Abilities: Starting new churches or pioneering new work.
Opportunities: Missions, evangelism, discipleship.
Warning: Be accountable to others.
Reward: Establishing new ministries that grow.
Prayer: Dear God, keep my eyes on You, not on my vision. For You are always more important than what I do for You.

Craftsmanship & Communication Perspective

CRAFTSMANSHIP
Abilities: Working with hands to make things that glorify God.
Opportunities: Missions, construction, choir, and drama (sets and
      props).
Warning: Don't become proud of personal ability and become
      difficult to work with.
Reward: Seeing God work through you to make things that bless
      others who don't have your gift.
Prayer: Dear God, help me to always be available to create things
      that others can't, in order to help them become more
      successful.

CREATIVE COMMUNICATION
Abilities: Unique ability to communicate God's truth through
      drama.
Opportunities: Drama, choir, evangelism, media, and missions.
Warning: Don't seek the spotlight or attention from others.
Reward: See God shine through you to help others
      understand His messages.
Prayer: Dear God, keep my eyes on You and not the crowd,
      so that I always do what I do for Your glory and not mine.

Discernment & Encouraging Perspective

DISCERNMENT

Abilities: Special insight concerning good and evil.
Opportunities: Counseling, prayer, and personnel.
Warning: Guard against quick judgments.
Reward: Protecting others from poor decisions.
Prayer: Dear God, give me a meek and quiet spirit, so that I can share Your truth in love and not with pride.

ENCOURAGING/EXHORTING

Abilities: Share practical steps of action.
Opportunities: Counseling, crisis center, and evangelism.
Warning: Choose words wisely.
Reward: Seeing people respond to your advice and helping them through problems.
Prayer: Dear God, use me to say what You would have me to say, not what I feel at the moment.

Evangelism & Faith Perspective

EVANGELISM

Abilities: Comfortably share the gospel with results.

Opportunities: Visitation, outreach, and missions.

Warning: Don't think everyone should be as dedicated to evangelism as you are.

Reward: Leading people to Christ glorifies God.

Prayer: Dear God, increase my vision for the lost, while helping me to understand why others do not share my burden.

FAITH

Abilities: Unique ability to trust God and His Word for the impossible.

Opportunities: Prayer, counseling, finances.

Warning: Believe as if everything depends upon God, but work as though everything depends upon you.

Reward: Influencing others to increase their faith.

Prayer: Dear God, increase my faith, while I increase my work for You. Don't let me become lazy.

Giving & Healing Perspective

GIVING

Abilities: Using stewardship to further God's Kingdom.

Opportunities: Finance or planning committee, and other office duties.

Warning: Don't use money to control others.

Reward: Knowing you contributed to the advancement of ministry without any personal recognition.

Prayer: Dear God, use my success with finances to bless the ministry and others.

HEALING

Abilities: Unique ability to pray for and help others be healed.

Opportunities: Prayer, hospital, hospice, and visitation of shut-ins.

Warning: Believing God wants to heal everyone exactly when you think they should be healed.

Reward: Seeing God heal people whose only hope was your help.

Prayer: Dear God, use me to help those who need the healing that only You can provide.

Hospitality & Intercession Perspective

HOSPITALITY

Abilities: Welcoming people into your home.

Opportunities: Homeless, encouragement, and housing.

Warning: Balance your family and personal needs with constantly inviting people to your home.

Reward: Giving others a comfortable rest and time of fellowship.

Prayer: Dear God, help me to work as hard at being close to You as I do at being hospitable.

INTERCESSION

Abilities: Being able to pray earnestly and faithfully for others.

Opportunities: Prayer, encouragement, hospital, hospice, and visitation of shut-ins.

Warning: Don't neglect other responsibilities.

Reward: Seeing how God answers prayer even after a long time.

Prayer: Dear God, show me how to balance my prayer life with the other responsibilities that I have in my life.

Interpretation & Knowledge Perspective

INTERPRETATION
Abilities: Unique ability to translate what others speak in tongues.

Opportunities: Encouragement, prophecy, counseling, and worship.

Warning: Don't interpret out from under your leadership's authority.

Reward: Blessing others by making unclear messages understood.

Prayer: Dear God, help me to make words spoken in tongues clear and positive so that others will grow in Christ, rather than bringing any glory to me.

KNOWLEDGE
Abilities: Ability to remember many things, especially from the Bible.

Opportunities: Counseling, work in the bookstore, and church library.

Warning: Don't get puffed up with much knowledge.

Reward: Helping others learn things they never knew.

Prayer: Dear Lord, You are the all-knowing One. May I only know and share what You show me. Help me not to be proud of the knowledge You have given to me.

Leadership & Miracles Perspective

LEADERSHIP
Abilities: Obvious influence to motivate others.
Opportunities: Men's or women's ministries, discipleship,
and support groups.
Warning: Lead by example, not just motivation.
Reward: Developing leaders to take over what you have done.
Prayer: Dear God, make me a strong and sensitive leader. Help
me to be well-balanced!

MIRACLES
Abilities: Unique faith to experience supernatural occurrences.
Opportunities: Prayer, finances, hospital visitation, and
encouragement.
Warning: Don't just believe in God being able to perform
miracles, but be responsible for personal commitments.
Reward: Seeing God work miracles that others thought
impossible.
Prayer: Dear God, keep me humble so that I never think I have
special powers apart from You.

Pastor/Shepherd & Prophecy Perspective

PASTOR/SHEPHERD

Abilities: Ministering to groups needing leadership.

Opportunities: Committee chairperson, visitation, care-group leader, and pastoral staff.

Warning: Don't get discouraged with those who don't follow.

Reward: Seeing the ministry improve.

Prayer: Dear God, help me be patient with those who are apathetic or spiritually weak.

PROPHECY/PERCEIVING

Abilities: Discerning right from wrong and declaring the truth.

Opportunities: Community/national concern, finances, and steering committee.

Warning: Don't be obnoxious or opinionated.

Reward: Helping others see the truth clearly.

Prayer: Dear God, give me the sensitivity to show love, while sharing truth that may offend.

Serving Ministry & Showing Mercy Perspective

SERVING/MINISTRY/HELPS

Abilities: Serving behind the scenes.

Opportunities: Nursery, Sunday school, and ushering.

Warning: Don't become weary of doing good.

Reward: Knowing you make a difference doing what no one else may want to do.

Prayer: Dear God, thank You for appreciating my labor of love, regardless of what others may fail to appreciate.

SHOWING MERCY

Abilities: Giving sympathy and/or empathy to the hurting.

Opportunities: Hospital visitation, benevolence, and counseling.

Warning: Don't be deceived. Ask God for wisdom and discernment as you work with others.

Reward: Knowing you helped those whom no one else would help.

Prayer: Dear God, use me to not only help people by showing care but also to share truth and tough love when necessary.

Teaching & Tongues Perspective

TEACHING

Abilities: Clarify truth/have insights as to why facts are true.
Opportunities: Teaching, training, and work in the church library.
Warning: Don't neglect other responsibilities.
Reward: Knowing people learn the truth.
Prayer: Dear God, help me to be practical, not to just research and impart truth.

TONGUES

Abilities: Unique ability to speak in unknown languages.
Opportunities: Prayer, counseling, encouragement, and worship.
Warning: Don't think everyone should speak in tongues as you do.
Reward: Encouraging others to grow in Christ as they commune with God.
Prayer: Dear God, help me to be sensitive to every situation and only speak in tongues when You want me to—not just when I "feel the spirit."

Wisdom Perspective

WISDOM

Abilities: Special insights to make wise decisions.

Opportunities: Prayer, counseling, finances, and conflict management.

Warning: Don't become proud of your wisdom.

Reward: Helping others make good decisions.

Prayer: Dear God, may my wisdom always come from You and not my own judgment. Help me to always rely on Your Word and not my opinions.

God sometimes calls us to do things we don't feel gifted to do. Moses was obviously not as gifted as Aaron with his communication skills. But God used Moses in a great way to lead the children of Israel out of Egypt.

Then Moses said to the LORD, "O my Lord, I am not eloquent, neither before nor since You have spoken to Your servant; but I am slow of speech and slow of tongue."
So the LORD said to him, "Who has made man's mouth? Or who makes the mute, the deaf, the seeing, or the blind? Have not I, the LORD?
"Now therefore, go, and I will be with your mouth and teach you what you shall say."
But he said, "O my Lord, please send by the hand of whom-ever else You may send."
So the anger of the LORD was kindled against Moses, and He said: "Is not Aaron the Levite your brother? I know that he can speak well. And look, he is also coming out to meet you. When he sees you, he will be glad in his heart.
"Now you shall speak to him and put the words in his mouth. And I will be with your mouth and with his mouth, and I will teach you what you shall do." Exodus 4:10-15

God has a special place of service and blessing for every Christian. We need to find where He is working and get involved. We also need to find where God has given us a burden of service to bear. Sometimes He gives us a burden that doesn't match our giftedness. However, this burden becomes a passion that can override our giftedness. We may not be gifted with communication skills, but our passion to help someone, or a group, can cause us to get involved.

Anyone can be a servant leader. Your giftedness and DISC

personality type is not most important. It's your relationship with God and others that makes the difference.

God doesn't always call the qualified, but He always qualifies the called!

Our natural motivations can also be overridden by our supernatural spiritual gifts. For example, you may have the gift of showing mercy, but your D personality may cause you to demand that others also show mercy.

Your interest in ministry may seem more and sensitive, but you have a drive and determination to get the job done. You may feel compelled to serve in a ministry that shows mercy, but your personality makes you want to take charge and dominate others.

You may come across as being strong and insensitive, but your sincere spiritual motivation can be misunderstood. People may accuse you of not showing mercy to those you lead. Likewise, you may think they are not showing the mercy they ought to show.

Seek to be all things to all people. Ask God to help you respond to others the way He would have you respond, rather than letting your motivations control you.

Involvement from a Personality Perspective

Just as spiritual gifts function more effectively in specific ministries, so do certain personality types fit best in particular ministries in a church setting. It's like putting round pegs in round holes. A good fit is comfortable and powerful.

Most churches struggle because there are so many members, as round pegs, not fitting in square holes. They are uncomfortable, less effective, and often frustrated. Rather than enjoying the ministry, they have to endure their ministry in the church.

It's like building a house. You can't have all carpenters and no electricians, plumbers, or roofers. Specialization is always best. Finding the right people for each job is more practical and effective.

Some laborers are multi-talented, but most people tend to do best when they focus on perfecting one task. So it is in the body of Christ. The church tends to be most effective when its members focus on what they tend to do best—what they are most gifted to do.

Study the following personality types, each with its distinct abilities, opportunities, warnings, rewards, and suggested prayers. Specifically, focus on your personality type, and ask God to help you learn how you are called to serve.

"D" Perspective

"D" BEHAVIOR
(Active/Task-oriented)

Abilities: Lead, take stand, confront issue, persevere, dictate, make decisions, control.

Opportunities: Organize needed ministry, chair stewardship committee, head usher's committee, commit to specific challenge.

Warning: You want to control everyone, but must first control yourself. Remember, to have authority, you must be under authority. Be loyal to your leaders.

Reward: Follow your spiritual leaders. Allow Christ to be the Lord of your life, and God will use you in a great way to move the ministry forward.

Prayer: Dear God, control my driving, demanding, and dominant personality so I can be a strong and peace-making leader for Your glory.

"I" Perspective

"I" BEHAVIOR
(Active/People-oriented)

Abilities: Communicate, inspire, influence, and make friends, optimism, and enthusiasm.

Opportunities: Give public testimony, drama, social committee, greeter, encourager, discussion group leader, do visitation.

Warning: You naturally outshine others. Don't serve purely through your "personality." Also, indulging in pride and sinful lusts will destroy your testimony.

Reward: God designed you to shine for Him. When you allow Him to shine through you, He will use you in greater ways than you ever imagined.

Prayer: Dear God, keep me humble to do Your will, not mine. Help me give You and those who praise me the credit for all You have done.

"S" Perspective

"S" BEHAVIOR
(Passive/People-oriented)

Abilities: Support, serve, specialize, and finish what others start. Work behind the scenes, and do what needs to be done.

Opportunities: On call whenever needed, hospital visitation, encourage new members, work in office, keep records, telephoning and counseling.

Warning: Shyness hinders your opportunities to do great things for God. Be more aggressive and assertive. Be careful: people may take advantage of you.

Reward: Believing God's promise that you can do all things through Him who strengthens you, step out and try the difficult. You may be surprised by what God can do.

Prayer: Dear God, I know You use the weak things to confound the mighty and I often don't feel capable of serving You, but through Your grace I will.

"C" Perspective

"C" BEHAVIOR
(Passive/Task-oriented)

Abilities: Analyze, improve, discern, calculate, follow directions, do the right thing.

Opportunities: Finance committee, long-range planning, office, record information, research, teach, organize and order curriculum.

Warning: Due to your cautiousness, criticism comes easy. Don't always be pessimistic and hard to convince. Increase your faith in God and trust those you follow.

Reward: Ministers need competent people to fulfill their visions. You can be a great blessing if you continually look at the possibilities, rather than impossibilities.

Prayer: Dear God, help me be optimistic in the midst of problems—a source of encouragement to those who find faith and victory difficult.

I never grew more in my Christian life than when I first got involved in my church. When I was around 15 years old and attending a small Community Christian Church in Miami, Florida, I trusted Christ as my Savior. When I first began to attend the youth group meetings, I didn't know anything in the Bible. I had been raised as an atheist, my dad was a Communist, and later, he became a spy for Cuba's Fidel Castro.

My turning point!

I was led to Christ through the witness of my teenage friend, Bud Tickle. (His real name is "Harry" Tickle.) I always thought that his unusual name was interesting, because my name was also unique. My first name, Mels, was a family secret and stood for "Marx, Engles, Lenin, and Stalin." My dad was very creative, but my heavenly Father had a plan for my life that superceded everything my earthly father had planned.

The summer after I became a Christian, someone paid my way to camp at Bibletown in Boca Raton, Florida, and it is there that I dedicated my life to Christ. My whole life was changing. My little church, along with an independent youth ministry called "Youth Ranch," made a major impact on my life.

I committed myself to be a disciple of Christ and follow Him by serving in my church. The first thing one of the church leaders, Joann Crowder, asked me to do was to lead singing in Junior Church. I didn't even know all the songs, but each week, I learned them from the kids and I grew more and more.

Then, as a high school senior, I was asked to teach the junior high Sunday school class. I was learning the Bible like never before and growing more each year. Most of the six students in my class knew the Bible better than I did, but that did not matter. God was in the process of teaching and preparing me for a lifetime of Christian service. From my way of thinking, it certainly seemed as though I was growing more than the others in the class.

Therefore, it is easy for me to say that getting involved in the ministry of my church made all the difference in my spiritual growth. It was also so exciting and fun, plus such a blessing. I grew greatly in Christ because I obeyed Him and got involved. Without a doubt, it was one of the happiest times of my Christian life.

In our next lesson, we're going to look at choosing who and where you will serve.

Choose You This Day Whom and Where You Will Serve

Jewel 10

Discovering your spiritual giftedness could be one of your greatest adventures of all time! There are many challenges every Christian is called to meet, such as praying regularly, witnessing boldly, and so on. Don't let the lack of a specific spiritual gift or personality type discourage you from doing what the Lord commands you to do through His Word. Discovering your spiritual gift/s and personality type should never be an excuse for not doing what God has given you to do.

In fact, you even may be compelled to be involved in other ministries not suitable for your giftedness. Your giftedness is not as important as your obedience to Christ and if you are following Him, He will lead you to a place where you can serve Him and others.

The most important ministry is to be His follower and disciple-maker. Scripture reminds us that "the things that you have heard from me among many witnesses, commit these to faithful men who will be able to teach others also" (2 Timothy 2:2).

The best model of biblical discipleship is teaching others, who teach others, who teach others, who teach others, etc. Getting involved in the ministries of your church is a vital part of discipleship. You really can't be a true disciple and follower of Christ unless you are involved in a ministry.

There also are times of rest and sabbaticals when people set aside time to wait on the Lord for direction. But some people may have problems with finding a ministry or two, because they haven't yet recognized or gained an understanding of their giftedness.

Choosing where to be involved can be easy!

First, pray that God will give you wisdom about how your specific personality, spiritual gifts, talents, interests, and experiences relate. The Lord may direct you to get involved in ministries that don't seem to fit your "giftedness." Sometimes your passions and interests reveal a call to be involved in unrelated areas. God can use you in a great way as you allow Him to do His work through you.

The most practical way to discover where to serve is to consider the ministries that need your personality and spiritual gifts. For example, you may have an S-type personality with the gift of ministry/serving. Look for an opportunity to serve behind the scenes doing those things most people don't want to do—such as the kitchen work or putting books back on the shelves in the library. You can receive deep satisfaction knowing God uses you to meet special needs. Always remember that Moses had S-type tendencies by not wanting to be up front, but God used him as a great leader.

If you're an I-type personality with the gift of evangelism, you may want to get involved in a more active and aggressive outreach opportunity. S-types prefer more passive friendship- or relationship-type evangelism.

D-types with the gift of prophecy serve effectively in a community awareness type ministry, such as a campaign against pornography or battling a serious moral issue. These types prefer to perceive and declare truth.

Before you make a decision, review all the opportunities listed with your specific personality and spiritual gifts in mind. You may know of other opportunities not listed here. You may want to consider your experiences, interests, and passions. For example, you may not have an I-type personality with the gift of evangelism, but do have a burden to win the lost. However, your passion and experience will make you fit well in an evangelism ministry.

Communicate with the appropriate ministry leader. Notify him or her about your personality type, spiritual gifts, talents, interests, experiences, and passions. Ask for counsel concerning where others may think you fit best. Scripture teaches, "In the multitude of counselors there is safety" (Proverbs 11:14).

Fitly Joined Together

The following are opportunities for ministry in relationship to spiritual gifts. With your gifts, passions, and interests in mind, look at all the ministries available. You should also consider other ministries in your community not listed on the following pages.

If you are already involved in a ministry that doesn't seem to match your profile, don't think you automatically shouldn't be involved. Remember Moses!

Your past and present experiences should also enter into your search for a good fit. In summary, consider your spiritual gifts, personality type, interests, passions, and experiences in making your choices. Find your specific primary and secondary spiritual gifts on the following pages. Read through the list to see if a ministry or two appeals to you. Then get involved as soon as possible.

Study the following suggestions to see where your spiritual gift or gifts fit best as you seek to serve the Lord as an obedient disciple in your church.

Administration/Ruling

Accounting, benevolence, clerical, construction, counseling, deacons, discipleship, elders, finances, foods, grounds, kitchen, library, long range planning, mailings, maintenance, meals, media, men's ministry, missions, newsletter, personnel, physician, prayer, printing, publicity, records, refugee/homeless, search committee, security, single parents

Apostleship/Pioneering

Big Brothers, coaching, college/career, construction, deacons, discipleship, elders, evangelism, high school, ethnic ministry, intercessory prayer, junior-high, long range planning, martial arts, media, men's ministry, missions, nurse, personnel, physician, recreation, script reader, security, song leader, search committee, senior adults, single adults, steering committee, trustees, visitation, women's ministry

Craftsmanship

Adult choir, Big Brothers, carpentry, coaching, construction, deacons, discipleship, drama, elders, evangelism, ethnic ministry, intercessory prayer, long range planning, maintenance, martial arts, media, men's ministry, missions, nurse, personnel, physician, recreation, Scripture reader, security, setup, song leader, search committee, steering committee, trustee, visitation, women's ministry, yard work, youth choir

Creative Communication

Choir, band, Big Brothers, coaching, college/career, communication, concerts, counseling, deacons, discipleship, drama, elders, encouragement, evangelism, high school, junior high, Internet Web site, media, men's ministry, newsletter, nurse, prayer, printing, receptionist, Scripture reader, single parents, sound ministry, tape ministry, teaching, trustees, video

Discernment

Accounting, counseling, deacons, discipleship, elders, finances, intercessory prayer, newsletter, personnel, physician, prayer, printing, publicity, records, search committee, secretarial, security, setup, small groups, sound system, steering committee, supplies, tape ministry, tutoring, transportation, trustees, ushers, vehicles, video, visitors' cards, writing

Encouraging/Exhorting

Altar counseling, adult choir, band, Big Brothers, choir, coaching, college/career, communication, concerts, counseling, deacons, discipleship, drama, elders, encouragement, evangelism, high school, hospice, hospital, junior high, media, men's ministry, newsletter, nurse, prayer, receptionist, Scripture reader, single parents, tape ministry, teaching, trustees, video, worship

Evangelism

Altar counseling, Big Brothers, bowling, carpentry, cleaning, coaching, communication, concerts, construction, counseling, deacons, discipleship, drama, elders, electrical, evangelism, foods, greeters, high school, housing visitors, internet web site, junior high, kid's camp/VBS, martial arts, meals, media, men's ministry, missions, musician, newcomers, newsletter, nurse, trustees

Faith

Altar counseling, baptism, Big Brothers, clerical, college/career, communication, communion, counseling, curriculum, deacons, discipleship, elders, elementary, encouragement, evangelism, ethnic ministry, high school, intercessory prayer, junior high, media, men's ministry, missions, newsletter, personnel, prayer, preschool, publicity, Scripture reader, search committee, senior adults, single adults, trustees

Giving

Accounting, benevolence, bookstore, clerical, coaching, computer, construction, curriculum, decorating, deacons, discipleship, elders, electrical, emergency medical technician, finances, floral arrangements, foods, graphic arts, grounds, housing visitors, visitation, kitchen, library, long range planning, mailings, maintenance, meals, media, men's ministry, missions, musician, newcomers, trustees

Healing

Altar counseling, communication, counseling, deacons, discipleship, drama, elders, encouragement, evangelism, graphic arts, ethnic ministry, hospice, hospital, intercessory, prayer, media, men's ministry, missions, newsletter, personnel, photography, prayer, publicity, refugee/homeless, senior adults, shut-ins, single parents, supper club, trustees, weddings, women's ministry, worship

Intercession

Altar counseling, baptism, Big Brothers, clerical, college/career, communication, communion, counseling, curriculum, deacons, discipleship, elders, elementary, encouragement, evangelism, ethnic ministry, high school, intercessory prayer, junior high, media, men's ministry, missions, newsletter, personnel, prayer, preschool, publicity, Scripture reader, search committee, senior adults, single adults, trustees

Interpretation

Altar counseling, baptism, Big Brothers, clerical, college/career, communication, communion, counseling, curriculum, deacons, discipleship, elders, elementary, encouragement, evangelism, ethnic ministry, high school, intercessory prayer, junior high, media, men's ministry, missions, newsletter, personnel, prayer, preschool, publicity, Scripture reader, search committee, senior adults, single adults, trustees

Knowledge

Accounting, clerical, counseling, deacons, discipleship, elders, finances, newsletter, office machines, orchestra, personnel, physician, prayer, printing, publicity, records, search committee, secretarial, security, set up, small groups, sound system, steering committee, supplies, tape ministry, tutoring, transportation, trustees, ushers, vehicles, video, writing, yard work

Leadership

Big Brothers, coaching, college/career, construction, deacons, discipleship, elders, evangelism, high school, ethnic ministry, intercessory prayer, junior high, long range planning, martial arts, media, men's ministry, missions, nurse, personnel, physician, recreation, Scripture reader, security, song leader, search committee, senior adults, single adults, steering committee, trustees, visitation, women's ministry, youth, youth choir

Mercy

Bereaving, Big Brothers, carpentry, child care, children, cleaning, communion, construction, counseling, deacons, discipleship, elders, elementary, emergency medical technician, evangelism, foods, greeters, homeless, housing visitation, hospital, hospice, infants/toddlers, interpreting, intercessory prayer, kids camp/VBS, kitchen, meals, newcomers, nurse, nursery, physician, shut-ins, trustees

Miracles

Altar counseling, communication, communion, counseling, deacons, discipleship, drama, elders, encouragement, evangelism, ethnic ministry, intercessory prayer, media, men's ministry, missions, newsletter, personnel, prayer, publicity, refugee/homeless, senior adults, shut-ins, single parents, supper club, trustees, weddings, women's ministry, worship

Pastor/Shepherd

Altar counseling, baptism, Big Brothers, college/career, communication, communion, counseling, curriculum, deacons, discipleship, elders, elementary, encouragement, evangelism, ethnic ministry, high school, intercessory prayer, junior high, media, men's ministry, missions, newsletter, personnel, prayer, publicity, Scripture reader, search committee, senior adults, single adults, trustees

Prophecy/Perceiving/Proclaiming

Coaching, communication, construction, deacons, discipleship, elders, emergency medical technician, evangelism, finances, intercessory prayer, kitchen, long range planning, martial arts, media, men's ministry, newsletter, nurse, nursery, personnel, prayer, printing, records, Scripture reader, search committee, security, steering committee, sound system, tape ministry, teaching, trustees, visitation, women's ministry, writing

Serving/Ministry/Helps

Adult choir, altar counsel, band, baptism, bereavement, Big Brothers, bookstore, carpentry, child care, children, choir, cleaning, clerical, coaching, college/career, communion, concerts, construction, counseling, decorating, deacons, discipleship, drama, elders, electrical, elementary, emergency medical technician, encouragement, evangelism, floral arrangements, trustees

Tongues

Altar counseling, communication, communion, counseling, deacons, discipleship, drama, elders, encouragement, evangelism, ethnic ministry, intercessory prayer, media, men's ministry, missions, newsletter, personnel, prayer, publicity, refugee/homeless, senior adults, shut-ins, single parents, supper club, trustees, weddings, women's ministry, worship

Teaching

Accounting, bookstore, clerical, coaching, computer, counseling, curriculum, deacons, discipleship, elders, electrical, elementary, finances, Internet Web site, interpreting, library, men's ministry, missions, physician, prayer, printing, records, Scripture reader, search committee, security, steering committee, tape ministry, teaching, tutoring, trustees, video, women's ministry, worship, writing

Wisdom

Accounting, counseling, deacons, discipleship, elders, finances, intercessory prayer, men's ministry, newsletter, personnel, physician, printing, publicity, records, search committee, secretarial, security, setup, small groups, sound system, steering committee, supplies, tape ministry, telephone calling, tutoring, transportation, trustees, ushers, vehicles, video, visitors cards, women's ministry, writing

Keep in mind these lists are not complete. There are many other ministries that may fit each spiritual gift list. These lists also do not take into account the leading of the Holy Spirit or your specific passions.

There may be a ministry not even listed for any of the spiritual gifts. God may be leading you to start or encourage the starting of that particular ministry. Don't let the absence of a particular ministry you are looking for discourage you. In fact, it should excite you, because God may be using you to investigate and/or initiate the starting of that ministry.

Now study the following suggestions to see where your personality type might fit best to serve the Lord in your church.

D-Types

Carpentry, coaching, construction, deacons, discipleship, elders, emergency medical technician, evangelism, finances, media, men's ministry, missions, long range planning, personnel, publicity, prayer, recreation, search committee, security, steering committee, teaching, trustees, ushers, vehicles, worship, yard work

I-Types

Band, Big Brothers, bowling, choir, coaching, college/career, communications, concerts, counseling, deacons, discipleship, drama, elders, elementary education, evangelism, encouragement, greeters, graphic arts, high school, ethnic ministry, housing visitors, junior high, interpreting, kids camp/VBS, media, men's ministry, missions, music, newcomers, new members, orchestra, organ, photography, piano, prayer, publicity, Scripture reading, receptionist, recreation, secretary, senior adults, single adults, song leading, summer camp, supper club, support group, song leader, teacher, telephone calling, trustee, usher, video, visitation, women's ministry, worship, youth, youth choir

S-Types

Altar counselor, baptism, benevolence, bereavement, Big Brothers, bookstore, bowling, carpentry, children, child care, cleaning, clerical, college/career, communion, concerts, counseling, deacons, decorating, discipleship, elders, elementary, encouragement, evangelism, follow-up, foods, grounds, ethnic ministry, hospital, hospice, housing visitors, infant/toddlers, interpreting, intercession, prayer, kids camp/VBS, kitchen, library, mailings, maintenance, meals, missions, newcomers, new members, newsletter, nurse, nursery, office machines, orchestra, organ, physician, piano, preschool, printing records, receptionist, refugee/homeless, Scripture reading, search committee, secretary, senior adults, serving meals, set up, shut-ins, single adults, small groups, sound system, summer camp, supper club, supplies, support groups, tape ministry, teaching, telephone calling, tutor, transportation, trustees, ushers, vehicles, visitation, visitors cards, weddings, women's ministry, worship, writing, yard work, youth choir

C-Types

Accounting, band, benevolence, bookstore, carpentry, children, cleaning, clerical, communion, computer, concerts, construction, curriculum, deacons, decorating, discipleship, drama, elders, electrical, emergency medical technician, evangelism, finances, follow-up, food, floral arrangement, graphic arts, grounds, infants/toddlers, Internet Web site, interpreting, kitchen, library, mailings, long range planning, maintenance, meals, missions, music, newsletter, nurse, nursery, office machines, orchestra, organ, personnel, photography, physician, piano, prayer, preschool, printing, publicity, records, Scripture reader, search committee, secretarial, security, serving meals, set up, sound system, supplies, steering committee, tape ministry, teaching, transportation, tutor, trustee, vehicles, video, visitors cards, weddings, worship, writing, yard work

Everybody is somebody in His Body!

By now, I'm sure you are beginning to understand that every Christian needs be involved in a ministry. Your Christian service encourages spiritual growth. Also, you will quickly discover that joy and exercising your giftedness are related closely to one another, and that you will experience tremendous blessings as you minister to others.

Not only do you need to serve—the Church needs servants. Nearly every ministry lacks people who will give of themselves to help others. This is why believers should never hesitate to donate their time, talents, treasure, and temple as stewards of God.

Both you and the Church will benefit when every member becomes a minister. The following pages contain suggestions where you may "fit" best in serving the Lord. Completing the following *Opportunity for Ministry* survey is part of discovering your **SHAPE** for ministry.

Rick Warren, Pastor of Saddleback Church, has popularized the emphasis on discovering your **SHAPE**—"**S**" is for spiritual gifts; "**H**" is for heart (passion); "**A**" is for abilities (talents); "**P**" is for personalities; and "**E**" is for experience. These letters identify the ministries that make up your **SHAPE.**

Prayerfully review each opportunity on the following pages, keeping in mind your spiritual gifts, personality type, and passion. Place an "**E**" next to each area in which you have experience. Place an "**I**" in the areas you find interesting or have abilities in. Place an "**H**" in the areas where you have a heart or passion (where you are most excited) about that ministry.

Then choose three specific opportunities where you want to serve. Share the choices with your minister or a leader who can give you wise counsel. Ask him or her to help you find a special place of ministry where you can exercise your giftedness.

There are many other opportunities of ministry not listed. You may even want to start a new one. ***Grow for It!***

1. ___ Accounting
2. ___ Adult Choir
3. ___ Altar Counselor
4. ___ Band
5. ___ Baptism
6. ___ Benevolence
7. ___ Bereavement
8. ___ Big Brothers
9. ___ Bookstore

10. ___ Bowling
11. ___ Carpentry
12. ___ Child Care
13. ___ Children
14. ___ Choir
15. ___ Cleaning
16. ___ Clerical
17. ___ Coaching
18. ___ College/Career
19. ___ Communication
20. ___ Communion
21. ___ Computer
22. ___ Concerts
23. ___ Construction
24. ___ Counseling
25. ___ Curriculum
26. ___ Decorating
27. ___ Deacons
28. ___ Discipleship
29. ___ Drama
30. ___ Elders
31. ___ Electrical
Elementary
       32. ___ Sunday
       33. ___ Midweek
       34. ___ Special Events
35. ___ Emergency Medical Technician
36. ___ Encouragement
37. ___ Ethnic Ministry
38. ___ Evangelism

39. ___ Finances
40. ___ Floral Arrangements
41. ___ Follow-up
42. ___ Foods
43. ___ Graphic Arts
44. ___ Greeters
45. ___ Grounds

High School

      46. ___ Sunday
      47. ___ Midweek
      48. ___ Special Events

49. ___ Housing Visitor
50. ___ Hospitals
51. ___ Hospitality
52. ___ Hospice

Infants/Toddlers

      53. ___ Sunday
      54. ___ Midweek
      55. ___ Special Events

56. ___ Interpreting for the Deaf
57. ___ Intercessory Prayer

Junior High

      58. ___ Sunday
      59. ___ Midweek
      60. ___ Special Events

61. ___ Kid's Camp, VBS
62. ___ Kitchen
63. ___ Library
64. ___ Long Range Planning
65. ___ Mailings

66. ___ Maintenance
67. ___ Martial Arts
68. ___ Meals
69. ___ Media
70. ___ Men's Ministries
71. ___ Men's Softball
72. ___ Men's Basketball
73. ___ Missions
74. ___ Musician
75. ___ Newcomers
76. ___ New Members
77. ___ Newsletter
78. ___ Nurse
79. ___ Nursery
80. ___ Office Machines
81. ___ Orchestra
82. ___ Organ
83. ___ Personnel
84. ___ Photography
85. ___ Physician
86. ___ Piano
87. ___ Prayer
Preschool
       88. ___ Sunday
       89. ___ Midweek
       90. ___ Special Events
91. ___ Printing
92. ___ Publicity
93. ___ Records
94. ___ Receptionist

95. ___ Recreation
96. ___ Refugee/Homeless Ministry
97. ___ Scripture Reader
98. ___ Search Committee
99. ___ Secretarial
100. ___ Security
101. ___ Senior Adults
102. ___ Serving Meals
103. ___ Set up
104. ___ Shut-ins
105. ___ Single Adults
106. ___ Single Parents
107. ___ Small Groups
108. ___ Song Leading
109. ___ Sound System
110. ___ Steering
111. ___ Summer Camp
112. ___ Supplies
113. ___ Supper Club
114. ___ Support Groups
115. ___ Tape Ministry
116. ___ Teaching
117. ___ Telephone Calling
118. ___ Tutoring
119. ___ Transportation
120. ___ Trustees
121. ___ Ushers
122. ___ Vehicles
123. ___ Video
124. ___ Visitation

125. ___ Visitor Cards
126. ___ Weddings
127. ___ Women's Ministries
128. ___ Women's Softball
129. ___ Worship Leader
130. ___ Writing
131. ___ Yard Work
132. ___ Youth
133. ___ Youth Choir

Choosing ministries in order to be involved in your church is absolutely vital to your spiritual growth. It will also affect your joy and fulfillment as a believer. You should not neglect this responsibility and opportunity to serve the Lord through your giftedness.

Let this be the time when you actually choose up to three ministries you may want to be involved in. List them in order of your preference.

1. _____

2. _____

3. _____

The next important step in becoming a fully obedient follower of Christ is to share your interest and/or commitment with your minister or a church leader. Don't wait to be asked to get involved. Just show up and let the leader know you are there to serve. This is also a great way to see if the "chemistry" is right, and if you will feel comfortable serving in that particular ministry.

If you don't seem to fit in one place, don't become discouraged. Simply try another ministry to see if that one is right. God has a special place for you to serve. Therefore, don't let anything stop you from finding your place in ministry.

It will be your perfect place of service for the King of Kings!

You can now identify which ministry you may fit best by completing your Uniquely You Profile in the convenience of your own home or office. Go on the internet to ***www.myuy.com*** and click on UY Profiler for more information.

Review

Because this chapter is so important, I want you to seriously consider what you have just read. Take a moment to study the sections "Choose You This Day" and "Fitly Joined Together." Specifically pray that God will give you wisdom in deciding where you will serve. Remember, the question is not whether you should serve or not. The real question is "Where will you serve?"

There are numerous opportunities for ministry listed. Your church may have its own list of opportunities. Also, your minister or involvement coordinator can share specific ministries needing volunteers. Consider one to three of these ministries for possible involvement.

Decide now to get involved in the ministry of your church!

Now think about the responsibilities of the specific ministries you have chosen to consider. Ask your minister or involvement coordinator questions, such as, "When, where, and how much time will this ministry take? What would my specific duties be?"

Don't expect detailed answers, because most churches are not organized enough to provide thorough "job descriptions." This won't really matter to D and I personality types. However, those who are C-types may feel a little uncomfortable without the answers they think they need.

You may be interested in other ministries not listed in this chapter. God could also give you a burden or passion for a ministry you don't seem gifted to do. This study doesn't deal with calling, anointing, and maturity. Just like God led Moses, He may lead you to do something you don't feel qualified to do.

Be sure to let your spiritual leaders know about your desire. Be patient and pray that God will open the door for you to do what you really want to do. After all is said and done, it doesn't matter what your spiritual gifts or personality types are. Also, where you choose to serve is not the most important issue.

The only thing that truly matters is this: Does God have His way in your life? The key is yielding to the Holy Spirit's control. "Do you not know that to whom you present yourselves slaves to obey, you are that one's slaves whom you obey, whether of sin leading to death, or of obedience leading to righteousness?" (Romans 6:16).

Serving the Lord is serious business with God. Timid Moses wrote: "I call heaven and earth as witnesses today against you, that I have set before you life and death, blessing and cursing; therefore choose life, that both you and your descendants may live" (Deuteronomy 30:19).

The Choice Is Yours!

Growing in God's grace is not something that happens automatically. It is a choice. Every Christian must decide whether or not to be a disciple and grow in grace or groan in disgrace. It is not enough to just study the Bible and its practical application in our lives. And while discovering our giftedness is good, allowing God to use us when and where He chooses is the very best.

If you discover that you are not suited for a certain ministry, don't quit or get discouraged. Remember, God used Moses in a great way, in spite of his personality. Continue serving wherever you are, as unto the Lord and not unto man or self. Finish your commitment, and then prepare to engage in a new ministry. Pray that God will give you the wisdom you need for the future.

Study the following information and ask God to show how He wants to bless you for serving Him.

Joy and Giftedness

The words "joy" and "gifts" are related in the Bible. They both come from the same Greek root word—*charis*. Their connection has wonderful implications—real joy comes when we exercise our gifts. God divinely designed us with a plan and a purpose. His purpose was to bless us by our discovering and using our giftedness for His glory.

Discovering our giftedness is fascinating. However, we also need to keep our spiritual focus set on the main thing, which is to "glorify God with your body and spirit" (1 Corinthians 6:19-20). When we do this, we will reap the benefits of true joy because we have learned the secret of allowing God to use us in the way He designed us to be used.

In Romans, the apostle Paul admonishes us: "I beseech you therefore, brethren, by the mercies of God, that you present your bodies a living sacrifice, holy, acceptable to God, which is your reasonable service. And do not be conformed to this world, but be transformed by the renewing of your mind, that you may prove what is that good and acceptable and perfect will of God" (12:1-2).

If you really want to discover God's will for your life, give Him your giftedness along with your feelings, thoughts, and actions. Allow Him to use you both naturally with your personality and supernaturally with your spiritual gifts.

The Bible teaches us not to be like children tossed to and fro, all mixed up in life. Instead we should "speak the truth in love, may grow up in all things into Him who is the head—Christ" (Ephesians 4:15).

We all need to mature in Christ, so we can enjoy life as God intended!

Dedicate your giftedness to God. He wants to bless you more than you could ever imagine. Remember that happiness is a choice. You will experience true joy, *charis*, when you are exercising your giftedness, but you also must make a commitment to be used by the Lord.

Don't wait for anyone to ask you to get involved. As stated earlier, start THIS WEEK by just showing up and saying, "I'm ready to serve!" Don't be surprised if things are a little disorganized and chaotic at times. Remember, the Day of Pentecost was one of the most confusing but glorious days of all!

These insights should help you understand where you fit best in ministry. Never forget, every member is a minister! This could be your Day of Pentecost, when God pours out His blessings on your life and uses you in ways you never dreamed. But it also could be a nightmare because of people. Serve God, regardless of whatever conflicts and clashes you may have, and you will be blessed.

Keep your eyes on Christ and you will succeed!

Avoiding and Resolving Conflicts

Jewel
11

Whenever two or more people work, worship, or live together, there will eventually be differences of opinions. This is not to say there will always be conflicts. Clashes usually occur because people have their own ways of thinking, feeling, and acting, plus have difficulty finding a harmonious way of talking and working with others who have different attitudes.

Most problems in ministry are not theological or technical. They are more relational. Therefore, we must understand and practice biblical resolution management. The Bible is clear concerning what we should do whenever we have a conflict with someone.

The greater the number of people involved in ministry, the more chances exist for conflicts. As maturing Christians, we must understand how group dynamics create potential conflicts. Unfortunately, many Christians avoid conflicts by avoiding involvement in ministry.

Imagine how exciting it must have been the morning of the Pentecost! It was the "birthday" of the Church (if you agree theologically). It is one of the greatest days in the history of humankind. God poured out His Spirit on all believers.

If you had volunteered to help on that day, you probably would have been excited, nervous, and even confused. This was a major Jewish festival, and thousands of people were pouring into Jerusalem.

Imagine being in charge of parking and hearing people complain, "There's not enough donkey spaces for everyone!" Or imagine being in charge of the sound system. The sound in the room where the disciples were praying was like that of a mighty rushing wind. It was loud, and more than most could handle.

What if you were in charge of ushering? Where would you have put all those people? Surely, crowd control was difficult. What if you were in charge of interpreting? There were people from every language and nation. It was impossible to handle.

Imagine the confusion and chaos there must have been. If you were a volunteer, how would you have responded? Would it have been too much to handle? But it was the "birthday" of the Church! God was doing a work that has never been duplicated since.

D- and I-type personalities must have loved it. S- and C-types would have been frustrated. Those with the gifts of prophecy and exhortation were excited, while those with the gifts of administration/ruling, teaching, and giving must have had serious doubts and questions.

When God does a great work, there is often confusion and disorganization. We cannot humanly keep up with what God does miraculously. When God blesses a church in a supernatural way, there will usually never be enough workers, finances, or facilities, but that's what miracles are all about.

When Jesus fed the five thousand

Imagine what it must have been like when Jesus told the disciples to feed the five thousand. Thomas must have freaked out. He no doubt thought, "This is crazy. We only have five loaves and two fishes. Jesus has gone too far this time!"

Most churches are crippled from lack of faith and vision. Too many S and C personalities are not willing or ready for change. D and I personalities also add to the problem by not being patient and loving enough to wait for their brothers and sisters in Christ to adapt and change.

The exciting reality is that God has not finished with us. (Philippians 1:6) As we obey and serve Him through our churches, He is conforming us into His image. Before the foundations of the world were formed, God knew who would trust Him as Savior. He predetermined that all who believed in Him would also be conformed into His image. Once we become Christians, our greatest desire should be for God to conform and change us into His image. Paul writes, "For whom he did foreknow, he also did predestinate to be conformed to the image of his Son, that he might be the firstborn among many brethren" (Romans 8:29).

Being conformed into Christ's likeness involves becoming controlled by His will and way. Even though the way we feel and think has definitely been influenced by our past, it does not have to control us. Happiness is a choice that we make. We can allow our personalities and spiritual gifts to control our flesh or we can control our giftedness for God's glory.

The bottom line is that we must guard against selfish responses. Better yet, we must allow the Holy Spirit to be master of our temperaments—to temper and strengthen us for His glory.

When we do this, God will use our spiritual gifts way beyond what we ever imagined.

How to Handle Conflicts

One of the greatest, if not the greatest, hindrances to spiritual growth is conflict. Excited Christians, desiring to serve God, are often discouraged because of misunderstandings and clashes with other Christians.

The following insights are designed to help you discover why people do what they do under pressure and why you may get into conflict with others. Scripture is clear on how to handle clashes. The problem is many Christians are not aware of their "sensitive spots." Believers also need to learn what the Bible teaches about resolving conflicts.

Every personality has its "hot button." When pushed too far, each one of us, regardless of our temperament, can act like a D-type personality. The following are tendencies of personalities as they relate under pressure.

One of the things I stress to those who are seeking to get a grasp on runaway emotions is, "Seek to be spiritual, not natural!" When frustration builds, stop and think about how God would have you respond.

Remember, most problems in the Church today are not theological. They are clashes between personalities and/or spiritual gifts. Each personality type and spiritual gifts has its specific way of responding and reacting. The following pages have insights on how different spiritual gifts tend to respond under pressure, their sources of irritations, and what needs to be done when conflicts come. Study these insights to learn how your specific motivations tend to affect you. Also, consider how you may respond differently from your "giftedness."

.

The following are basic thoughts and not intended to be conclusive. Prayerfully consider what you do, then search the Scriptures and good biblical counsel, plus your own heart and mind, before you respond in a conflict with anyone.

Gifts of Prophecy, Apostleship, and/or Miracles

Under Pressure:
>   Becomes dictatorial, domineering, demanding, angry, intense, forceful, direct, bossy

Sources of Irritation:
>   Weakness, indecisiveness, and laziness. Lack of discipline, plan, purpose, direction, authority, control, and challenge

Needs to:
>   Back off, seek peace, relax, think before reacting, show self-control. Learn to be patient, loving, friendly, loyal, kind, and sensitive.

Gifts of Encouragement, Creative Communication, and/or Faith

Under Pressure:
> Becomes hyper, overly optimistic, immature, emotional, irrational, silly, wordy, and selfish

Sources of Irritation:
> Disinterest, slowness, pessimism, details, time restraints, antagonism, doubt, structure. Lack of enthusiasm, and team participation

Needs to:
> Listen, count the cost, control emotions. Learn to be humble, strong, disciplined, punctual, careful with words, and conscientious.

Gifts of Mercy, Healing, and/or Intercession

Under Pressure:
> Become subservient, insecure, fearful, weak-willed, withdrawn; a sympathizer and a sucker

Sources of Irritation:
> Pushiness, instability, inflexibility, anger, disloyalty, insensitivity, pride, discrimination, and unfairness

Needs to:
> Learn to be strong, courageous, challenging, aggressive, assertive, confrontational, enthusiastic, outgoing, expressive, cautious, and bold.

Gifts of Giving and/or Wisdom

Under Pressure:
> Becomes picky, judgmental, sensitive, intense, manipulative, and vulnerable

Sources of Irritation:
> Waste, stinginess, insensitivity lack of discipline, willpower, direction, and determination; also a lack of stewardship, control, challenge, and concern

Needs to:
> Learn to be more flexible, patient, risky, understanding, forgiving, and discerning so that he or she will not be taken advantage of.

Gift of Evangelism

Under Pressure:
> Becomes hyper, talkative, pushy, intense, forceful, direct, bossy; doesn't listen well

Sources of Irritation:
> Apathy, indecision, laziness, all talk and no do, lack of concern for the lost, challenge, inactivity, purpose, direction, leaders who are not good examples

Needs to:
> Back off, slow down, relax, minister to needs of others, and build relationships. Learn to be patient, loving, friendly, kind, and sensitive.

Gifts of Teaching, Discernment, and/or Knowledge

Under Pressure:

Becomes too serious, haughty, high-minded, critical, contemplative, judgmental, moody, and analytical

Sources of Irritation:

Shallowness, inaccuracies, disorganization, lack of preparation, validation, plan, direction, authority, control, and depth

Needs to:

Relax, build relationships, ask more questions, allow for discussion, and spend more time being practical. Learn to be friendlier, funny, upbeat, and enthusiastic.

Gift of Pastor/Shepherd

Under Pressure:

Becomes serious, insensitive, overly concerned, nosy, intense, regimented, overbearing

Sources of Irritation:

Spiritual weakness, indecisiveness, immaturity, lack of discipline, plan, vision, direction, power, control, and consistency

Needs to:

Serve by example, build relationships, relax, think before reacting, and control self. Learn to be more patient, loving, kind, considerate, and tolerant.

Gifts of Serving/Ministry and/or Hospitality

Under Pressure:

> Becomes selfless, sacrificing, weak-willed, cooperative, sympathetic, and sensitive

Sources of Irritation:

> Inconsiderateness, inactivity, anger, and disloyalty, lack of volunteers, help, and concern

Needs to:

> Be challenging, aggressive, assertive, bold, enthusiastic, expressive, delegating, creative, confident, and leading.

Gifts of Administration/Ruling, Interpretation and/or Leadership

Under Pressure:

> Becomes moody, critical, contemplative, negative, and worrisome

Sources of Irritation:

> Incompetence, disorganization, foolishness, dishonesty, inaccuracy, wastefulness, inconsistency, blind faith, and false impressions

Needs to:

> Loosen up, communicate, and be joyful, positive, tolerant, compromising, open, trusting, and enthusiastic.

Now let's look at DISC personality types under pressure, their sources of irritations, plus what they need to do when conflicts come. These insights are basic thoughts and not intended to be conclusive. Prayerfully consider what you do, then search the Scriptures, good biblical counsel, plus your own heart and mind before you respond in a conflict with anyone.

"D" Behavior

Under Pressure:
Becomes dictatorial, domineering, demanding, angry, intense, forceful, direct, and bossy

Sources of Irritation:
Weakness, indecisiveness, laziness; lack of discipline, plan, purpose, direction, authority, control, and challenge

Needs to:
Back off, seek peace, relax, think before reacting and control emotions. Be more patient, loving, friendly, loyal, kind, and sensitive.

"I" Behavior

Under Pressure:
> Becomes hyper, overly optimistic, immature, emotional, irrational, silly, wordy, and selfish

Sources of Irritation:
> Disinterest, slowness, pessimism, details, time restraints, antagonism, doubt, rigid structure, lack of enthusiasm or team participation

Needs to:
> Listen, count the cost, control emotions. Be humble, strong, disciplined, punctual, careful with words, and conscientious.

"S" Behavior

Under Pressure:
> Becomes subservient, insecure, fearful, weak-willed, withdrawn, a sucker

Sources of Irritation:
> Pushiness, instability, inflexibility, anger, disloyalty, insensitivity, pride, discrimination, and unfairness

Needs to:
> Be strong, courageous, challenging, aggressive, assertive, confrontational, enthusiastic, outgoing, expressive, cautious, and bold.

"C" Behavior

Under Pressure:

> Becomes moody, critical, contemplative, negative, and worrisome

Sources of Irritation:

> Incompetence, disorganization, foolishness, dishonesty, inaccuracy, wastefulness, inconsistency, blind faith, and false impressions

Needs to:

> Loosen up, communicate. Be joyful, positive, tolerant, compromising, open, trusting, and enthusiastic.

Predictable patterns of behavior are especially evident when we are under pressure and stress. Our natural responses are easily seen. I highly recommend you consider the following as you deal with your most difficult relationships.

Natural Responses to Conflict

D —	Wants to attack
I —	Wants to expose others
S —	Wants to support or submit
C —	Wants to criticize

Recommended Wise Responses

D	—	Restore with love
I	—	Make others look good
S	—	Care enough to confront
C	—	Examine own self first

Some people may believe that these insights are too simple. They may argue that human behavior science is more complicated. They often want to dig deeper and understand all there is to know about the subject of behavior. But keep in mind, we often respond to any study based upon our own personality types.

C-type individuals can't get enough information. They want to learn everything, while D-types want a quick and simple summary. I-types want to discuss, while S-types often take your word for everything.

The most important need in this study is to apply what we learn to our everyday lives. It really doesn't matter how much we learn, but how we apply it. The greatest lesson we can learn is how our behavioral types control and change our lives for God's glory.

Help your church members to learn more about *how to avoid and resolve conflicts* by identifying and understanding their spiritual gifts and personality types. Encourage them to go to our Web site at *www.myuy.com* and click on UY Profiler for more information. It is a wonderful blessing when church members "serve the Lord with gladness."

Now let's look at leadership insights from a DISC perspective.

Leadership Insights

Almost everyone responds to life's challenges and choices according to his or her personality. Therefore, individuals who want to understand their relationships with others must be personality-wise.

For example, high-I leaders should not engage high-D followers in small talk. D personality types prefer leaders who get to the point. They want "bottom line" answers, and they respond best to those who are not going to waste their time.

On the other hand, high-S followers feel comfortable with leaders who are systematic, slower, and steady in their approaches. S-types don't like fast talking, quick-paced responses.

The following is an overview of two different types of leadership theory. There are many theories about what makes a good leader. This is simply my opinion based upon my years of experience, plus much personal research.

Take a moment and ask yourself, "Am I a transactional or transformational leader?"

So what's the difference?

According to many authorities on leadership there are two fundamental types of leaders: the transactional and the transformational. Transactional leaders engage in an exchange process with followers; "If you do this, I'll give you that." Transformational leadership, by contrast, gets people to do far more than they themselves expect they can do."

Transactional leadership is more contingent upon rewards. There's a contract exchange of rewards for tasks. There are promises of rewards for good performance. Accomplishments are recognized. There's a transaction between the leader and the follower.

On the other hand, transformational leadership is inspirational. It provides vision and purpose. Followers are offered something more than rewards. There's a relationship based upon healthy pride, respect, and trust, rather than just accomplishments and rewards.

Transformational leaders have charisma. They communicate high expectations that transform followers and organizations. These type leaders often overcome the problems that arise from the misunderstandings about leadership.

Everything rises or falls on leadership!

Regardless of what type leader you are, understanding the science of leadership is imperative. Leadership is the backbone — the heart and soul, the hands and feet that make things work best. Without good leadership, an organization is like a ship without a rudder. It's like an airplane without wings, or like an archer without arrows. Transformational leadership is more than just leading.

Transformational leadership is a lifelong process of "becoming" — of being transformed in order to transform others. It's not natural traits enabling leaders to be better than others. People actually learn and grow into more effective leaders.

According to Bass and Stogdill, there is "devastating evidence" against the traits theory of leadership. "A person does not become a leader by virtue of the possession of some combination of traits, but the pattern of personal characteristics of the leader must bear some relevant relationship to the characteristics, activities, and goals of the followers."

Everyone is born a leader!

You may have heard that people are born leaders. Or maybe you have heard that leaders are not born, they are made! I believe everyone is born a leader. Consider newborn babies. Their slightest sound makes us jump.

My Down's Syndrome brother-in-law, Dickie, who lived with us up to his death at 60 years old, had the mind of a six-year-old child. Yet, he was a leader. Everyone is and can become a leader. That's what transformational leadership is all about—being transformed by the renewing of your mind to become what you were designed to be.

Becoming a transformational leader begins by recognizing you are endowed to succeed in life. Fulfilling that purpose can transform you into a blended (DISC) servant leader!

The most effective leaders are transformational servant leaders. They understand themselves and others and work on a higher plain of life. They discover the insights that transcend the norm or typical. They learn how and what it takes to impact others.

Understanding human behavior science and applying what you learn can help you identify your style of leadership. The Uniquely You Leadership Personality Profile identifies your DISC personality type. Simply adapt what you learn to leadership from a servant leader perspective. The interpretation and practical application throughout the profile will help you clearly see the relationship between personality types and transformational servant leadership.

Hopefully this study will result in better attitudes, improved relationships, and measurable results. Identifying your DISC profile from a leadership perspective can be the beginning of a new way of leading for you and others.

It can make the difference in happiness and sorrow—success and failure in life. These insights can help you discover and develop the unique leader within you!

Next we will take a moment to describe the different leadership styles. I have found that people tend to lead according to their personalities, rather than adapt to the styles of others.

The following pages are basic insights taken from the DISC Leader's and Follower's Styles.

D & I Leader's Styles

"D" Leaders

D personality types are "take control and be in charge" types. They don't like people telling them what to do. D leaders can be too pushy and forceful. They need to control their direct and demanding approach to management. They make better leaders when they learn to slow down, be gentle, and not be so demanding of others.

"I" Leaders

I personalities are inspiring and enthusiastic. They love to lead and influence others. Naturally great presenters, they tend to talk too much. I-type leaders need to listen more and not be so sensitive to rejection. They are the most impressive and positive leaders. They love crowds, but need to be interested in individuals.

S & C Leader's Styles

"S" Leaders

S leaders are sweet, steady, and stable leaders. They seldom demand anything. They are friendly and loyal, but tend to be too nice. They need to be more aggressive and assertive. Overly sensitive to their shortcomings, S leaders need to be more confident. They hate to take risks. They often miss opportunities because of their caution. Reliable and relaxed, they are more reserved.

"C" Leaders

C leaders are competent and compliant. They go by the book and want to do everything just right. They are thorough and detail-oriented, but tend to be too informative. C personalities need to be more positive and enthusiastic. They answer questions people aren't asking. When optimistic, C leaders are extremely influential. They should not concentrate on problems, but focus on potentials.

D & I Follower's Styles

People also follow according to their personalities. Identifying our individual followers' styles makes leaders more effective.

"D" Followers

D personalities respect strong leaders. They want to be part of a winning team. They follow with power and authority in mind. They wonder, "Will this action make me more respected and/or get the job done?" D followers need choices, rather than "get in or get out" ultimatums. They need opportunities to do their own thing.

"I" Personality Followers

I personalities follow with their hearts. Therefore, they tend to be impulsive followers. They want opportunities that will make them look good. They also talk a lot. They make great first impressions. Their high egos and ability to persuade often turn them into the leaders in order to rise to the top. Sometimes you don't know who's leading whom.

S & C Follower's Styles

"S" Followers

S followers don't make quick decisions. They like leaders who are understanding and gentle. They want to establish relationships with a leader who will be around for a long time. S personalities are concerned about service and stability. When it comes to sensible and slow judgment, this personality type feels right at home. They like familiar and low-key environments.

"C" Followers

C type personalities are *Consumer Reports* type followers. They analyze each decision and love research and development. They are quality oriented followers. They don't like quick or costly decisions. Picky and precise, they follow with their minds, rather than their hearts. C-types seldom respond positively at first. They often want time to think about their decisions. Once convinced, they follow best.

Learning to lead means we first learn how to follow. To be a good leader, we must learn to be a good follower.

The most effective leader is the blended servant leader!

Blended servant leaders learn how to adapt and become "all things to all men." They understand that people are rarely as objective as they would like to be. Everyone is informed and motivated by their specific personality. They guard their strengths from overuse, and improve or "perfect" (2 Corinthians 12:9-10) their "uniquenesses/weaknesses."

Blended servant leaders allow the Holy Spirit to control their drives, passions, and wills in order to motivate others more wisely. Servant leaders are transformational leaders who raise people up to follow on a higher plain.

Anyone can be a servant leader. Your giftedness and DISC personality type are not most important. It's your relationship with God and others that makes the difference.

God doesn't always call the qualified, but He always qualifies the called!

In our next lesson, we're going to look at *Biblical Resolution Management*.

Biblical Resolution Management

Jewel 12

Once you get involved in ministry, conflicts will come. First of all, Satan, our enemy, wants to divide us. He also wants to discourage us and keep us from serving God. In fact, once we accept Christ as our Savior, this becomes his principle concern—to keep us from doing God's will. Peter understood this truth and warns us to "be sober, be vigilant; because your adversary the devil walks about like a roaring lion, seeking whom he may devour" (1 Peter 5:8). He is committed to destroying our relationships with those we love, especially our relationship to the Lord. Therefore, we must guard our hearts and minds with God's truth, which is found in His Word.

Another point that we need to consider is that there are times when God allows conflicts to come into our lives to make us stronger. We may think that trials and difficulties are the enemy's handiwork. While he may be the one causing the confusion, God is the only One who promises to bring good out of our sorrow, trouble, and misfortune. (Romans 8:28) He takes a crooked stick and points a straight path. He takes the trials of life and turns them into testimonies. He takes our greatest hurts and turns them into opportunities for us to grow in Christ.

Certainly, the apostle Paul knew what it meant to face severe opposition and persecution. In 2 Corinthians, he writes, "And He said to me, My grace is sufficient for you, for My strength is made perfect in weakness. Therefore most gladly I will rather boast in my infirmities, that the power of Christ may rest upon me. Therefore I take pleasure in infirmities, in reproaches, in needs, in persecutions, in distresses, for Christ's sake. For when I am weak, then I am strong" (12:9-10).

Since conflicts are one of the most challenging problems in our Christian growth, we need to know what God's Word has to stay about conflict resolution.

A Biblical Resolution Management Covenant helps church members avoid and resolve conflicts. Every church should use this to improve their people problems. Churches are very weak in this area. Business and industry are better at resolving problems than churches are. Yet churches have the best "how-to" manual—the Bible! This is our greatest source of truth and godly instruction. It is in the pages of God's Word that we learn how to deal with our differences.

Prayerfully and carefully read through the following covenant. As you do, ask the Lord to show you how to deal with conflict when it comes from a godly perspective.

Covenant

In obedience to God's Holy Word and commitment to practicing biblical resolution management, I promise to follow the Principle of Priorities. That is, my priorities are to glorify God, build harmony in the church, and avoid conflict. I will do as Matthew 18 admonishes: go to an offending brother "first alone."

First Step

I will not first share the offense with another person. I am committed to restoring the relationship, rather than exposing possible sin. I recognize most problems with people are personality clashes, and I will try to understand their actions based upon their perspective.

Second Step

If going to a person "first alone" does not resolve our differences, I promise to seek a neutral and mature individual who will listen to each of our perspectives of the problem. This person will hopefully be able to shed light on one or both of our blind spots or areas of needed growth in order to glorify God.

I recognize that the "witness" may reveal or say things I won't like, but I will believe God is using him or her to resolve the conflict, rather than take sides. (The "witness" must be an individual with deep spiritual wisdom and highly respected by all those involved.)

Warning

I will not seek to find others who have also been offended, nor share my concerns with potential "witnesses" prior to the meeting with my "offending brother." The purpose of having a "witness" is not to validate my hurt but rather to open my heart and mind to the possible needs I may have regarding my relationship with others.

I realize my friends may naturally listen to my concerns, but also take up my offense. I will, therefore, not cause them to become a party to a possible division and disharmony because of our friendship. Whenever I feel an urge to share the offense with my friends, I will pray and commune with God about my hurt.

Confronting Ministry Leaders

I believe in the scriptural admonition to not rebuke an elder (spiritual leader), other than in grave matters of misconduct and open sin. "Do not receive an accusation against an elder except from two or three witnesses" (1 Timothy 5:19).

I will earnestly pray for and follow those God has placed in leadership over me. I will not allow anyone to criticize them without following the principles in Matthew 18 and without the specific person present.

If I have a problem with my ministry leader, I will go "first alone" to him or her. I will not share my concern with anyone. I will listen and try to understand his or her perspective of the problem. If I am not satisfied with the explanation and continue to have animosity, I will ask permission and counsel to find a "witness" who will listen to our conflict.

If the "witness" finds I have misunderstood the situation

and should continue no further, I will trust God to complete His work in my life by casting my burden on the Lord and leaving it there. If the "witness" agrees with my concern and finds the ministry leader wrong and the leader refuses to hear the "witness," we will then find a group of two or three other "witnesses" who will hear the matter and determine what God is doing through this conflict.

Serious Step

If I continue to find fault with a ministry leader and cannot worship in "spirit and truth," I will seek to join another ministry rather than cause any conflict and disharmony. I am committed to pleasing God through resolving my conflicts, even if it means separating myself from the source of my irritations.

Ultimate Goal

I commit myself to be spiritual rather than "normal," and supernatural rather than "natural," when it comes to solving my problems with others. I want God's will and way to resolve my conflicts and will do as the Holy Bible teaches, regardless of my normal and natural feelings.

My ultimate goal is to glorify God through bearing much fruit, getting involved in ministry, and avoiding and resolving conflicts.

Review the *Biblical Resolution Management Covenant* step-by-step. Also share this covenant with the leadership of your church. Above all, be committed to giving a "good report" and resolving conflicts from a biblical standard.

Unfortunately, this happens all the time!

When I was a pastor in Florida, one of our leaders came
to me and said there was a problem. He had seen the car of one of
our active church members in the parking lot of a porno store. He
stopped at the gas station across the street to wait and see if the
member would come out of the store.

After a while, sure enough, there he came. The leader
couldn't believe it. He came to me very upset. I told him not to tell
anyone, but to go to the member "first alone." The serious question
here is, "Do we want to expose our brother or do we want to
restore our brother?"

Most of what is done in the church today is to expose our
offending brothers. We ought to weep whenever a brother or sister
falls into temptation and sins. It ought to break our hearts when we
see "sin in the camp."

I think there is something dark and dirty (old sin nature) in
all of us that tempts us to expose our fallen friends. I also believe
there is something psychological that makes us feel better when
we can point out the faults of others. It's the "beam in your eye"
(Matthew 7:3-5) problem we all can have.

When the leader went to his friend to confront him, the
member first responded defensively and asked, "Have you told
anyone?" When the leader could honestly say no, because he didn't
tell me who it was, the member began to cry.

I'm convinced that if the leader had said, "Yes, I told the
pastor, or my prayer partner, or my wife," that the member would
have not responded well. When the member realized that the leader

really cared about him and had come to him "first alone," the member began to weep. He confessed he had a problem and had been praying that God would send someone to help him.

When we deal with problems in the church, especially with fellow members and their problems, we need to resolve these conflicts biblically by going to our brothers and sisters "first alone" and giving them a chance to explain. Sometimes it "isn't as it seems to be." The member could have gone in the porno place to drag a friend out.

I've gone into a bar to pull someone out. Critics could have judged me and started a rumor based upon the "facts" as they saw them. We need to be "quick to hear and slow to speak" (James 1:19). We also need to care enough to confront. However, the care we need to have should be that of reconciliation rather than condemnation.

You won't believe this!

One night, a pastor went to an elders meeting where he was confronted by the church board members. Their demand was simple: he could resign or be fired. He was told that being "fired" wouldn't look good on his resume.

He was blindsided. He had no idea this was coming. However, the fact was that a couple of weeks before the meeting he had heard from another pastor, who also was a friend, that one of his elders was talking to another pastor to see if he might be interested in being the new pastor!

This was obviously upsetting, because the current pastor did not know of any problems. When he asked the chairman of the board if there was anything he needed to know, the chairman assured him that there were no problems. The chairman actually lied or, at best, misled his pastor. There were problems, and none of the elders cared enough to confront their pastor. They waited for a surprise attack that would devastate this unsuspecting shepherd.

He regretfully resigned and told his wife that he felt led of the Lord to leave the church. Their lives were never the same. He decided never to pastor again but continues to serve the Lord with these awful memories.

Why couldn't the board of so-called godly men come to their pastor and explain the problem in advance? Why did they sucker-punch him?

I believe it was a power struggle. The church had nearly tripled in size in only two years. There were no moral accusations, no legal problems, and no doctrinal issues. There were definitely personality conflicts and spiritual gifts clashes.

Failure

The board of elders and pastor had failed to communicate and/or learn the importance of biblical resolution management. Unfortunately, this story is familiar in churches all over the world. Sadly, it is said that Christians are the only ones who bury their wounded.

There are countless stories of ministers, leaders, Sunday school teachers, and church members who have been fired or released from their duties without knowing why. These things should never happen.

Never listen to anyone who wants to talk about another brother or sister in Christ behind his or her back. We should have the right to face our accusers and cross-examine them in order to hear the evidence that is brought against us. We should have our day in court, but very few churches in the world follow this pattern.

Church Court

I know of one church that follows this pattern. It is Oak Cliff Bible Fellowship, where Dr. Tony Evans is pastor. They have "Church Court" where members can present their problems with other church members before a respected mediating board that is committed to helping them resolve their conflicts. This is how we should deal with conflicts in the church. We shouldn't have to go to secular court and present our "dirty laundry" before the rest of the world.

Ironically, the United States has the best judicial system in the world because of biblical influences. William Blackstone, a highly respected English jurist, used the book *English Common Law,* from which our forefathers took many of their principles, to establish our American judicial system. Blackstone believed in and used the Holy Scriptures to form the backbone of his writings. Therefore, we have the best court system in the world because of the Bible.

Despite the foundations of our civil law, the church today is so ignorant or just plain disobedient of biblical conflict resolution principles that it is no longer "like a mighty army [that] moves the Church of God." We're more like a "wounded tortoise, treading where we've always trod."

Why are we so poor at fighting the enemy and so good at fighting each other? Within the church, we have many horrible casualties of "friendly fire" as we seem to kill our own soldiers. Often the arrows of our fellow soldiers who are behind the front line shoot their arrows into the backs of front line soldiers — fatally wounding the most valuable warriors.

When are we going to learn that we are "fellow soldiers" with a specific enemy? Someone has said, "We've found the enemy, and we are it!" That may be poor grammar, but it is a wise insight. We need to take all this conflict in the church more seriously.

God hates discord. Sadly, many churches are crippled because of disharmony. Churches would be stronger and much more effective if their members would determine to abide by biblical resolution management principles.

Once you get involved in ministry, conflicts are inevitable. When we face conflict with others, we must constantly remember that our ultimate goal is to glorify God!

The Bible commands us to "put on the whole armor of God, that ye may be able to stand against the wiles of the devil. For we wrestle not against flesh and blood, but against principalities, against powers, against the rulers of the darkness of this world, against spiritual wickedness in high places.

"Wherefore take unto you the whole armor of God, that ye may be able to withstand in the evil day, and having done all, to stand. Stand therefore, having your loins girt about with truth, and having on the breastplate of righteousness; and your feet shod with the preparation of the gospel of peace; above all, taking the shield of faith, wherewith ye shall be able to quench all the fiery darts of the wicked.

"And take the helmet of salvation, and the sword of the Spirit, which is the word of God" (Ephesians 6:10-17).

We must also desire to restore our offending brothers and sisters, rather than exposing them. Keep in mind that our battle armor only covers the front of our bodies (helmet of salvation, sword of the Spirit, breastplate of righteousness). There is nothing to protect our backs.

Help your church members have their personal biblical resolution covenant with God. Help them identify and understanding their spiritual gifts and personality types in order to avoid and resolve conflicts more effectively. Encourage them to go to our Web site at ***www.myuy.com*** and click on UY Profiler for more information. Learning about our giftedness will create more unity in the body of Christ.

In the next lesson we are going to focus on our *Call for Commitment*.

Call for Commitment

Jewel 13

If the "main thing is to keep the main thing the main thing," then we need to make sure that we know what is the "main thing" is. Let's never forget that it is to "glorify God with your body and spirit" (1 Corinthians 6:19-20).

Scripture also admonishes us to "present your bodies, living sacrifices to God . . . to discover what is that good and acceptable will of God" (Romans 12:1- 2). If you really want to discover God's will for your life, you must give God your giftedness. Give Him your feelings, thoughts, and actions, both naturally with your personality and supernaturally with your spiritual gifts.

The Bible teaches us to not be like children, tossed to and fro, all mixed up in life. (Ephesians 4:14) Instead we should "speak the truth in love that we may grow up in Christ" (Ephesians 4:15). We all need to mature in Christ so that we can enjoy life as God intended.

From whom the whole body fitly joined together and compacted by that which every joint supplieth, according to the effectual working in the measure of every part, maketh increase of the body unto the edifying of itself in love." Ephesians 4:16

Your church may have provided you with tremendous learning experiences through these lessons, which are so important. Everything, however, would be wasted if you ended this study without being determined to be involved in a specific ministry, or if you did not learn how to avoid and resolve conflicts based upon biblical resolution principles.

I want to encourage you to consider making a commitment to follow Christ as your Savior and Lord. Dedicate your giftedness to Him, and you will experience His peace and joy. Also, you need to know that He wants to bless you more than you could ever imagine. Remember—happiness is a choice! True joy or "charis" comes when you exercise your giftedness.

Success or Failure

Success in the Christian life comes as you discern, obey, and yield to the Holy Spirit's will. Allow Him to be the Lord of your emotions, will, and thoughts. God can control your personality better than you can. He wants to live His life through you. Actually, you can't live the Christian life apart from Him. Only Christ can live the Christian life in you. You must allow Him to be the Lord of your life.

I am crucified with Christ: nevertheless I live; yet not I, but Christ liveth in me: and the life which I now live in the flesh I live by the faith of the Son of God, who loved me, and gave himself for me. Galatians 2:20

You can live the crucified life through Christ. Paul writes, "I can do all things through Christ who strengthens me" (Philippians 4:13). The difference between this truth and humanism is that the humanist would stop the verse after the word "things"—"I CAN DO all things!" A biblical view of human behavior science begins with God—"In the beginning God created"—and ends with CHRIST—"I can do all things through Christ."

Be all that you can be. You can do all things through Christ. But "whatsoever you do, do it heartily as unto Christ and not unto men" (Colossians 3:23). And "whatsoever things you do, do all to the glory of God" (1 Corinthians 10:31).

God gifted you to glorify Himself. He also has blessed you to benefit the church and others.

James admonishes us to remember, "every good gift and every perfect gift is from above, and cometh down from the Father of lights, with whom is no variableness, neither shadow of turning. Of his own will begat he us with the word of truth, that we should be a kind of first fruits of his creatures. Wherefore, my beloved brethren, let every man be swift to hear, slow to speak, slow to wrath: for the wrath of man worketh not the righteousness of God. Wherefore lay apart all filthiness and superfluity of naughtiness, and receive with meekness the engrafted word, which is able to save your souls" (James 1:17-21).

Discovering our giftedness is good, but exercising our gifts is even better. We need to obey all the Scriptures, not just the ones that are convenient or easy. The Bible tells us: "But be ye doers of the word, and not hearers only, deceiving your own selves" (James 1:22).

One of the greatest questions we face is, "Will I or will I not obey God?" Many Christians think that living a good life, being faithful in church attendance, and contributing their tithes will satisfy God. Beyond all that, we must be faithful in everything He has commanded us to do. Otherwise, we fall short of His will and often suffer the consequences of our so-called "little" disobediences.

> *Go to now, ye that say, today or tomorrow we will go into such a city, and continue there a year, and buy and sell, and get gain: whereas ye know not what shall be on the morrow.*
> *For what is your life? It is even a vapor, that appeareth for a little time, and then vanisheth away. For that ye ought to say, If the Lord will, we shall live, and do this, or that. But now ye rejoice in your boastings: all such rejoicing is evil Therefore to him that knoweth to do good, and doeth it not, to him it is sin.*
> *James 4:13-17*

Once you have completed this study, you should have a better idea of where you fit best in ministry. The information you have learned should help you understand yourself and others better, but don't stop here. Go on to maturity, involvement, and a more harmonious ministry.

Be sure to get with your pastor or involvement coordinator and find your special ministry in the church. Get involved ASAP. Also make a commitment to biblical resolution management.

The Bible is a book of principles. If we obey those principles, we will be blessed. If we disobey or neglect God's principles, we will suffer the consequences. God will honor and bless you when you decide to serve Him.

> *If any man serve me, let him follow me; and where I am, there shall also my servant be: if any man serve me, him will my Father honor. John 12:26*

Above all, allow God to use your giftedness for His glory!

Conclusion

Many people today are trying to become "one with the universe"! Or they are trying to "find themselves." The only way to find true happiness and become "one" with creation is to become "one" with the Creator. Our "wholeness" will be determined by what we do with God and His Word. Wholeness only happens when God is in control of our whole selves—spirit, soul, and body. (2 Thessalonians 5:23) To become whole we must begin with how and why God made us.

The Bible teaches that God made everyone unique!

God made our giftedness a priority in creation. In fact, everyone is gifted in unique ways. "Every man has his proper gift of God" (1 Corinthians 7:7). God gives gifts to us so that we might be the "first fruits of His creation" (James 1:18).

We are obviously very special to Him. The psalmist reminds us, "It is He who has made us and not we ourselves" (Psalm 100:3). Scripture also reveals that we are "wonderfully made" (Psalm 139:14).

Our giftedness reveals the unique way we think, feel, and act. It's the way God made or wired us. We all have God-given personalities that affect our natural motivations. As Christians, we also have one or more spiritual gifts that influence our supernatural motivations. Identifying our giftedness can be exciting and enlightening.

Not only are you gifted supernaturally with a specific spiritual gift, God also gifted you with natural motivations. You were conceived with a special personality. You were "born again" with unique spiritual gifts. Once you trust Christ as your Savior, you receive one or more special ways of thinking, feeling, and acting. Personality types are your natural way of responding. Spiritual gifts are divine enablements and endowments that make you a valuable part of the body of Christ.

No one is an island or sufficient unto himself!

Everyone has different gifts. No one has all the gifts. God made us to need each other. Romans 12:3 teaches, "Don't think more highly of yourself than you ought," because God made each part of the body to function separately, yet dependent upon the rest of the body.

Identifying our spiritual and natural giftedness leads to understanding our function within the church. God wants to bless and benefit us by using our giftedness for His glory. Therefore, we need to identify and use our spiritual gifts to enjoy life as God intended.

Ephesians 4:11-13 confirms that God gave gifts to Christians and gifted Christians to the church "for the work of the ministry, edifying of the body and unity of the faith."

Relating our natural motivations (personality types) to our supernatural motivations (spiritual gift types) can be enlightening. Most personality types relate to specific spiritual gift types. As we have already seen, individuals with the gifts of serving or showing mercy often have S-type personalities.

D- and C-type personalities often have the gifts of prophecy or administration. Exhorters are often I- or S-types. The gift of teaching corresponds best to C behavior.

Sometimes God combines a specific personality with an unrelated spiritual gift. God is not in a box. He does what He pleases. The Lord sometimes gifts individuals with seemingly opposing endowments and enablements—differing natural and supernatural giftedness. This explains why some Christians are often confused and frustrated by their conflicting motivations.

God gifted you to glorify Himself and to bless you!

Many Christians are miserable because they don't understand how God wants to exercise His gifts through them. God's specific will is that every Christian honor and serve Him. We glorify Him best when He uses our giftedness in ministry. "If any man serve me, him will my father honor" (John 12:26).

Also, whenever two or more people work, worship, or live together, there will eventually be differences of opinions. This is not to say there will always be conflicts. Clashes usually occur because people insist on their own ways of thinking, feeling, and acting.

Scripture admonishes us: "And he gave some, apostles; and some, prophets; and some, evangelists; and some, pastors and teachers; for the perfecting of the saints, for the work of the ministry, for the edifying of the body of Christ: till we all come in the unity of the faith, and of the knowledge of the Son of God, unto a perfect man, unto the measure of the stature of the fullness of Christ: that we henceforth be no more children, tossed to and fro, and carried about with every wind of doctrine, by the sleight of men, and cunning craftiness, whereby they lie in wait to deceive" (Ephesians 4:11-14).

Most problems in ministry are not theological or technical.

They are more relational. Therefore, we must understand and practice biblical resolution management. The Bible is clear concerning what we should do whenever we have a conflict with someone.

The more people involved in ministry, the more chances for conflict. As maturing Christians, we must understand how group dynamics create potential conflicts. Unfortunately, many Christians avoid conflicts by avoiding involvement in ministry.

Once you have discovered your giftedness and determined to serve the Lord by exercising your giftedness, you need to make a commitment to be involved in the ministry of your church.

Once you make a commitment to let God use your giftedness for His glory and your spiritual growth, be sure to share your decision with the minister or a leader in your church.

Always remember,
God made you unique to
bless you and glorify Himself!

Now would be a great time to order your Uniquely You Profile (paper instrument) or go online at ***www.uyprofiler.com*** to complete your personal profile. You may also want to complete your *Spiritual Life Survey* online to see how you compare with 13 specific spiritual habits vital to your growth in Christ.

If this book has been a blessing to you, share it with your minister or a friend to help them experience the joy of ***discovering your giftedness!***

SPONSOR A SEMINAR IN YOUR CHURCH

If you have never attended one of our Uniquely You seminars, you owe it to yourself to view our website and take a look at our current seminar schedule (www.myuy.com), or better yet, schedule one of your own! That's Right! You can host a Uniquely You seminar for your church, at no cost to your church. Call Dr. Stan Ponz at 1-706-492-5490 for further information.

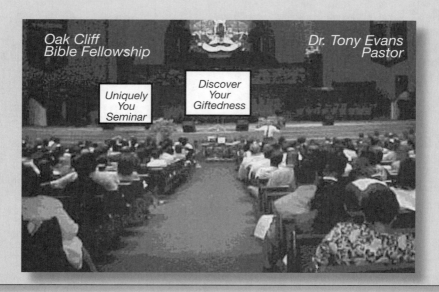

Uniquely You™ Resources
Christian Impact Ministries, Inc.
PO Box 490
Blue Ridge, GA 30513
e-mail: drmels@myuy.com
706-492-5490

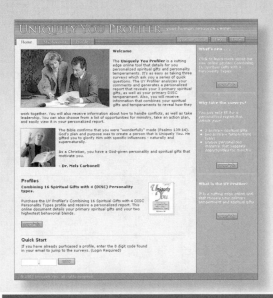
260

Three Ways

Biblical Human Resources Can Help You!

1 Uniquely You Online Certification Training

Become a Certified Trainer or Coach for churches, businesses, and/or schools!

Learn How To
Increase Involvement & Reduce
Conflicts from the convenience of
your phone and computer!

- Certified Church Assimilation Specialist (CCAS)
- Certified Leadership Training Specialist (CLTS)
- Certified Wellness Dynamics Specialist (CWDS)
- Certified Human Relations Specialist (CHRS)
- Certified Human Behavior Consultant (CHBC)

1, 2, or 3 Day Online
Certification Training

Basic, Specialist, and Advanced Training now available

Over 700,000 profiles now in print!

2 Sponsor a Discover Your Giftedness Seminar at no cost to your church budget!

Help your members get involved in the ministries of your church by identifying their Spiritual Gifts and 4 DISC Personality Types. Uniquely You will pay for all travel, lodging, materials, and honorariums if your church will simply promote and register a guaranteed number of people to attend the seminar.

Oak Cliff Bible Fellowship — Dr. Tony Evans Pastor
Uniquely You Seminar — Discover Your Giftedness

Presenters: Dr. Mels Carbonell, Dr. Stan Ponz,
or one of their Certified Trainers

Rick Warren, Pastor	Zig Ziglar, Author
Saddleback Church	"Dr. Mels Carbonell
"One of the best seminars ever!"	has a message America needs to hear!"

3 Leadership Hour or Wellness Hour Coaching Conference Calls

Receive personal coaching and consulting on various leadership, team building, health, and assimilation issues that will make a difference. Carbonell and Dr. Stan Ponz. Their nearly 70 years of combined experience in ministry can show you how to increase your effectiveness from a biblical Human Behavior Science perspective.

Mels Carbonell Ph.D.   Stan Ponz D.Min.

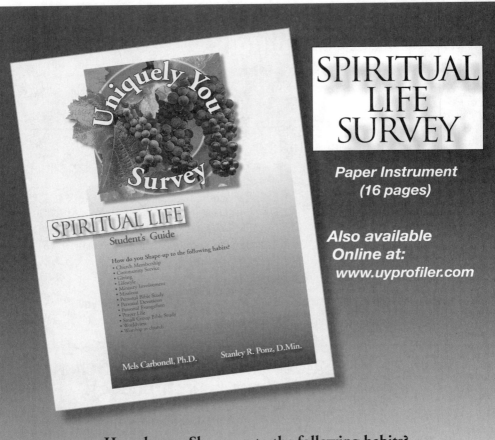